Center for Basque Studies
Basque Politics Series, no. 6

A Basque Patriot in New York

Jose Luis de la Lombana y Foncea and the Euskadi Delegation in the United States

Iñaki Anasagasti and Josu Erkoreka

Translated by Jennifer Ottman

Basque Politics Series, no. 6

Center for Basque Studies
University of Nevada, Reno
Reno, Nevada

This book was published with generous financial support from the Basque Goverment.

Basque Politics Series, no. 6
Series Editor: Xabier Irujo

Center for Basque Studies
University of Nevada, Reno
Reno, Nevada 89557
http://basque.unr.edu

Photos: All photos courtesy of the Archivo Iñaki Anasagasti

Cover and series design © 2013 by Jose Luis Agote.

Library of Congress Cataloging-in-Publication Data

Anasagasti, Iñaki.
 A Basque patriot in New York : Jose Luis Lombana y Foncea and the Euzkadi Delegation in the United States / Iñaki Anasagasti and Josu Erkoreka ; translated by Jennifer Ottman.
    p. cm. -- (Basque politics series ; no. 6)
 Includes bibliographical references.
 Summary: "A historical look at the work of Basque nationalist Jose Luis Lombana y Foncea and the Euzkadi Delegation in the United States in the years leading up to World War II"--Provided by publisher.
 ISBN 978-1-935709-38-1 (pbk.)
 1. Lombana y Foncea, Jose Luis, 1911-2001. 2. País Vasco (Spain)--Politics and government--20th century. 3. Spain--History--Civil War, 1936-1939--Governments in exile. 4. Euzko-Alderdi Jeltzalia--History--20th century. 5. Nationalists--Spain--País Vasco--Biography. 6. Basques--United States--Biography. I. Erkoreka, Josu. II. Title.

 DP302.B43L663 2013
 320.540946'6092--dc23
 [B]

                        2013012903

Contents

A *Jelkide* in New York

The relationship of the United States to the 1936 war is a story that has been told a thousand times, but almost always centered on the Lincoln Brigade, on the attitude of a number of famous intellectuals and artists, such as Ernest Hemingway, Lillian Hellman, or Philip Guston, or on the misgivings of the country's executive and legislative branches with regard to helping one side or the other.

Nevertheless, there are other stories, more local, nearer to hand, and more alive. Many of them took place in New York, the country's leading city and the site of contradictions of all kinds, from the actions of ethnic and national minorities, such as Hispanics, Germans, Jews, African Americans, Italians, and Chinese, to conflicts, which sometimes spilled out into the streets, between different religious faiths, with Catholics being absolutely in favor of Franco's rebels and Protestants supporting the Spanish Republic.

This is a complex history, one which was the subject of a March 2008 exhibit at the Instituto Cervantes in Alcalá de Henares, previously on view at the Museum of the City of New York. The 1930s were not the most prosperous of times for the city of skyscrapers. The stock market crash of 1929 led not only to the suicides of ruined investors but also to an unemployment rate of 25 percent, creating, logically, severe social tensions that particularly affected certain minorities.

In this atmosphere, news arrived from Europe that demanded a response. First came fascism and then Nazism, taking over Italy and Germany. In Japan, the Meiji Revolution had borne its fruits, and Japanese expansionism was in full swing. The outbreak of the Spanish Civil War on July 18, 1936, served as a catalyst for all these energies, and the supporters of one or another worldview radicalized their positions even further.

Notwithstanding historical conventional wisdom to the contrary, the supporters of aid to the Spanish Republic were in the minority among the press, all the more so when fascist and Catholic propaganda hinted that Spain risked becoming a Soviet satellite. At the same time, journalists covering the war sometimes adopted a policy of support for the current administration. For some, this undermined the credibility of their reports, as in the case of the great Herbert Matthews of the *New York Times.*

Intense Activity

The events in Spain sparked, if not frenetic activity, at least intense activity on the island of Manhattan. Solidarity meetings and demonstrations against the embargo imposed on Spain followed one upon another, as did, although to a lesser extent, demonstrations accusing the Republic of being anti-Christian and totalitarian, the majority led by parish priests and agitators such as Charles Coughlin. The recruitment of volunteers, many more of them unionized workers than romantic upper-class dilettantes (another myth in need of revision), is the best-known result of the Republic's propaganda efforts, but it was not the only one. Perhaps New York City's most significant contribution arrived in Spain in the form of ambulances and medical supplies, often accompanied by health professionals.

This Book

In the spare moments left by legislative business and while we searched the archives for information for a study of legislator Manuel de Irujo's parliamentary activity under the Republic, we discovered an unpublished report by a young *jelkide* (a Basque word referring to activists of the Basque Nationalist Party, EAJ-PNV for its Basque and Spanish acronyms) named José Luis de la Lombana. He had been the director of the newspaper *Euzkadi* in Barcelona and had been charged with attending the Second World Youth Congress for Peace in New York City in 1938.

We had never heard of this episode. Subsequently, this unknown Lombana lived in exile in Bogotá. We had only vague allusions to his activities and to the Basques' first steps in New York in trying to gain access to Catholic circles.

Since the subject was of interest to us, we began to research his life and to try to place into context a series of events that took place seventy-six years ago. This study adds to the knowledge of what happened in those years and the Republic's propaganda efforts in the United States relating to Catholicism and the Spanish Civil War. It brings to light the trip made by that intrepid young man, Lombana, who dared to travel to New York in the midst of war, without knowing a word of English, and to work with the

Spanish Republicans while maintaining a strongly nationalist position. It also documents his subsequent and complicated travels, full of hope, conviction, and a fair amount of naïveté, to various universities and academic institutions in the United States—an immense country—all in one year, 1938. In addition, it explores the relationships that existed in New York in 1938 between supporters of the Spanish Republic and Basque, Catalan, and Galician nationalists. It studies in depth the relationship between French Catholicism and the Basque Catholics and the EAJ-PNV's strategy for establishing a United States presence based in this sector of American society. Finally, it offers information about the difficult relationships among those who had to raise money for seemingly "lost" causes.

José Luis Lombana y Foncea, in his study.

In sum, our study aims to contribute to delineating the historical context of the events that took place in the United States, in Europe, and in Republican Spain at war; to reveal who José Luis de la Lombana was; to study the Roosevelt administration's non-intervention policy; to analyze the climate of confusion that dominated American Catholicism at the time; to describe the first steps taken by the Basque Government's delegation in New York, three years before the arrival of Lehendakari Aguirre, who escaped from World War II; to list the Republican and Basque organizations that were operating in those years; and finally, to present the Lombana Report, which speaks for itself and which we have simply ordered and supplied with an index.

Our work's novelty is its contribution to the study of an entirely unknown period, which has begun to receive attention thanks to the Basque Government's publication of *The Basque Archives: Vascos en Estados Unidos (1938–1943)* (*The Basque Archives: Basques in the United States (1938–1943)*) and to Koldo San Sebastián's book containing notes from Manu Sota's visits.

We would like to thank José Luis de la Lombana's daughter Miren, a resident of Bogotá, for the biographical information she provided about her father, in addition to documents from the archives of the Center for Basque Studies at the University of Nevada, Reno, and elsewhere. These documents revealed previously unknown information about Lombana's work in Barcelona and the Barandiaran Report subsequent to the fall of Gasteiz in 1936.

Patrick Sota, Manu Sota's nephew, supplied us with invaluable correspondence from this period, among which we would like to highlight the letter written by Lehendakari Aguirre to Fernando de los Ríos, the Spanish Republic's ambassador, as well as the letter written by the Basque Government's delegate, Antón Irala, to secretary Pedro de Basaldua, about the Lombana Report and the need to bring it to the Lehendakari's attention. It is possible that he did read it, since our copy contains a letter addressed to Lehendakari Aguirre, the text of which we reproduce. Finally, and with special thanks to Xabier Irujo who first tilled this ground, we would like to make known how in 1938 a young Basque nationalist advocated in New York for solidarity among all supporters of freedom and for peace to take root in the Old World of Europe.

José Luis de la Lombana y Foncea: An Active, Restless Man from Vitoria-Gasteiz; A Fervent Basque Patriot

José Luis de la Lombana y Foncea was born in Vitoria-Gasteiz on April 3, 1911. When he came into the world, his parents, Luis de la Lombana and Toribia Foncea Murguiondo, were living on the second floor at no. 32 Calle de la Estación, the house where he was born and the scene of his earliest childhood adventures.

The young José Luis attended primary and secondary school at the Marianist academy in the capital of the province of Araba (Álava). Intellectually gifted, with talents for both verbal facility and abstract reasoning, and gifted with a prodigious memory, he was an excellent student. His school vacations were generally spent in Kanpezu (Santa Cruz de Campezo in Spanish), also in Araba, the home of his mother's family. Lombana never forgot his childhood wanderings in that beautiful mountain locality. His spontaneous and untrammeled enjoyment of rural life infused Lombana with a profound sense of freedom that, in contrast to the rigorous order of his daily life in the city, he found enormously attractive. The surroundings of his childhood and youth, experienced with great intensity, were always a source of homesickness and longing for Lombana, a country boy at heart.

His early years, marked as they were by austerity, rigor, and work, as well as the customary education of that time, which promoted values such as discipline, hierarchy, and effort, forged a firm and decided personality in this man of brilliant intelligence and strong character. His personality was clearly reflected in his daily conduct, his path through life, and his relations with others.

After completing secondary school he began university studies, pursuing a degree in law and another in philosophy and letters (history section). His academic record indicates that he studied for his second degree at the University of Zaragoza, receiving his diplomas in Madrid. In 1931, José Luis obtained a business diploma (the degree of *profesor mercantil*), completing a varied and comprehensive university education.

Lombana as a graduate, c. 1930.

Although he is included in the 1932 list of licensed professionals of the Vitoria-Gasteiz bar association (Colegio Oficial de Abogados) as a non-practicing member, we know that Lombana remained connected to the academic world during a good part of the period coinciding with the Second Republic in Spain (1931–36). During that period he resided in Madrid, where he attended courses at the Universidad Central (Central University, now the Universidad Complutense) on the way to defending his dissertation to obtain a doctorate in law.

His excellent academic performance at the university did not prevent him from engaging in abundant cultural activities, nor was it an obstacle to the first demonstrations of his proverbial affinity for politics. He was only twenty years old when the Second Republic was proclaimed in April 1931, but his reaction was a clear and firm intention to take maximum advantage of the breath of freedom promised by the new regime. His formal membership in the Basque Nationalist Party (Euzko Alderdi Jeltzalea-Partido Nacionalista Vasco, EAJ-PNV) apparently dates from the first half of that year,[1] although his ties to organized Basque nationalism had begun under the dictatorship of Primo de Rivera (1923–30).

Despite living in the Spanish capital—where he was determined to receive a third degree—Lombana remained fully committed to politics and culture. His time living in Madrid did nothing to lessen the intensity of his convictions in favor of the Basque nationalist cause. On January 20, 1935, he was named president of Madrid's Eusko Ikasbatza (Basque Culture Group).[2] In his role as the association's head he went before the microphones of Radio Unión to introduce Aita Donostia (Jose Gonzalo Zulaika or "Father Donostia"), a renowned Basque musicologist who was visiting the city to give a lecture on the traditional Basque songs for St. Agatha's Eve (on the eve of St. Agatha's Day, February 5, it was customary for groups of people to go from house to house singing verses in exchange for small donations to various causes).[3]

In his natal city, Vitoria-Gasteiz, Lombana stood out from a very young age for the vigor of his Basque nationalist political activity. He emerged on the political stage through the auspices of the EAJ-PNV youth wing, where he made a name for himself with his dialectical skill, his capacity for work, and the radical nature of his commitment. The firmness of his political allegiance sparked some unsavory incidents in the capital of Araba, a polarized social environment steeped in political conflict.[4] More than one sticky

---

1. Santiago de Pablo, *En tierra de nadie: Los nacionalistas vascos en Álava* (Vitoria-Gasteiz: Ikusager, 2008), 151.

2. The purpose of the group, as certified by its secretary, Agustín Arraiza Lana, was "purely and exclusively scholarly" (Archivo Iñaki Anasagasti, Fondo Lombana).

3. *Euzkadi,* February 10, 1935.

4. Lombana told the story that upon arriving home one afternoon, he noticed that there were guests in the parlor, one of whom was a friend of his parents, a woman whose political opinions were contrary to his own and who was highly regarded in society. Lombana went past her without greeting her, surprising all who were present. When the lady inquired as to the reasons for his attitude, he answered, very calmly, that he had always believed that she only greeted hats, and since he had arrived wearing a beret. . . . He had scarcely finished the phrase when his father gave him a resounding clout in front of the guests. Later, however, in private, he explained the reasons for the correction: the argument used was correct, but it was neither the time nor the place for it.

situation arose that was provoked by the repression of Primo de Rivera's regime against political expressions of Basque nationalism.[5]

Staff of *El heraldo Álaves*, c. 1931. Lombana seated back row, far right.

During his youth, Lombana also took his first steps in the world of journalism and public relations. He worked initially as an editor for *El Heraldo Alavés*, an independent conservative and Catholic Vitoria-Gasteiz daily founded in 1901. After that paper closed in late 1932, he collaborated on editing the "Euzkadi in Araba" page that the EAJ-PNV's official daily paper began publishing in January 1933.[6] Lombana engaged in a notable level of propaganda activity, giving talks and lectures on a variety of Basque topics in a wide spectrum of forums.[7] Beginning in 1935, he joined the long list of lecturers used by the EAJ-PNV to promote the spread of Basque nationalist ideals.[8]

---

5. As in all military dictatorships, political activities were constantly repressed by (at times implacable) police raids. During one of these, Lombana was unable to escape the guards because he happened to be suffering from sciatica that prevented him from moving as he wished. He only managed to lean painfully against a post while everyone ran, fleeing from the police, and he ended up with a good beating. On recalling the event, however, he was in the habit of remarking with a laugh that the beating got rid of the sciatica, in what he called "wonders of the police therapy of that time."

6. Editor's note: Today the term Euskadi (with 's') is used to mean the Basque Country (generally the three provinces that comprise the Basque Autonomous Community, but also the wider meaning of the term), rather than Euzkadi (with 'z').

7. He saved with special care the invitations to two lectures: one given on April 8, 1935 in the salons of the Iberoamerican Union, Medinaceli 6, organized by the Basque Culture Group and New Bibliophiles as part of the events planned on the occasion of the Wilhelm von Humboldt centenary, addressing the topic of the Basque traditional laws and privileges (the *fueros*) as seen by the German author, and one given on September 14 at the Basque Book Exposition held at the palace of the Provincial Council (*diputación*) of Araba and organized by the Baraibar Society of Basque Studies group, on Samaniego and his times.

8. José María Tapiz, *El PNV durante la II República: Organización interna, implantación territorial y bases sociales* (Bilbao: Fundación Sabino Arana/Sabino Arana Kultur Elkargoa, 2001), 497.

The Military Uprising of July 18, 1936 and Its Effects in Vitoria-Gasteiz

According to Lombana's own account, given to anthropologist José Miguel de Barandiaran, it fell to Lombana to play a major role in the actions taken by the Basque nationalists in the capital immediately following the uprising of Franco's troops. On the same day, July 18, 1936, a confidential report reached Lombana through an aunt, a friend of the wife of the editor-in-chief of *El Pensamiento Alavés*. The report affirmed that "that night, before five o'clock in the morning, a military-Carlist-type movement was going to break out."[9] This movement would be important for Basque patriots because it was, in part, directed "against the nationalists," particularly Javier de Landáburu, a prominent figure in Basque nationalist circles in Araba. Landáburu had been an elected representative in the Spanish parliament for the province of Araba during the two "dark years" between 1933 and 1935 when a coalition of center-right and far-right parties ruled Spain.

As soon as he learned of this report, Lombana went to the premises of the EAJ-PNV's Basque Youth (Juventud Vasca) organization in Vitoria-Gasteiz, where he called a meeting with some of the best-known leaders of the party in Araba. The assembled nationalist activists deliberated with the care demanded by the seriousness of the situation. Lombana's opinion was categorical:

> I proposed that if the movement was a political one posing the issue between fascism and communism, we would do better with the latter, being less harmful to our cause, but I maintained that in Euzkadi, the choice between fascism and communism was not at issue, since communism did not exist, either as a majority or as an audacious minority. Therefore, I believed that in Euzkadi the issue was between fascism and democracy. In the religious aspect, we should support the legally constituted state, and in the event of rebellion, we should contribute to the defense of our people, maintaining moderation in that defense. Hence, our action had to be to make contact with the republicans and prevent military personnel from concentrating, and in addition, I proposed to them that they take control of the weapons stores, where I supposed that there were thirty-seven thousand rifles.

Lombana's plan obtained the support of those gathered, although, at Julián Aguirre's suggestion, it was agreed that action should be taken by the

9. José Miguel de Barandiaran, *La guerra civil en Euzkadi: 136 testimonios inéditos* (Milafranga-Villefranque: Bidasoa, 2005), 282.

party activists who participated in the meeting in their individual capacity, without involving the organization directly. In the end, the decision was made in an informal meeting among members who did not yet have the express and official endorsement of the party's highest authorities.

Despite the cautionary measures adopted, the Basque nationalist activists acted with all the haste demanded by the situation. They agreed to designate a commission, made up of Juan Ruiz, Jesús Ruiz de Angoitia, Martín Ortiz de Lafuente, and Lombana himself, to speak with the leaders of the Republican Center (Centro Republicano) and inform them of their plan. Nevertheless, the civil governor's unwillingness to give them the arms they requested and the chilly reaction of the republican activists themselves—who, according to Lombana, after several hours "remained skeptical of our attitude of alarm, to such an extreme that nothing better occurred to them than to post a note on the Circle's bulletin board calling a republican demonstration" for the next day—ended up unraveling the plan of resistance proposed by the Basque nationalists.[10]

Back at the Basque Youth premises, Lombana and his comrades felt that "the greatest possible sacrifice had to be demanded from our members, but on the basis of some guarantee in that regard, and never sending them into a fight made unequal by lack of resources, in which the future factionalists might tear them to shreds." For this reason, they issued an ultimatum. If they were not supplied with the arms they had requested by four-thirty in the morning, they disclaimed "all responsibility for whatever might happen," ordering the Basque nationalist activists to return home, "since it was not possible to act effectively."

The hours passed, and the weapons did not arrive within the established time. The civil governor lacked the courage to authorize their distribution to the people, even with the guarantee that their distribution and use would be rigorously monitored by the political organizations. Defeated by their powerlessness and feeling bitter, the Basque nationalists decided to withdraw: "When we realized the state of abandonment in which the authorities had left all the democrats," Lombana noted, "we ordered our two hundred or three hundred men, who were waiting for us, to go back home, since there was nothing that could be done, short of eliminating the governor, which it was not our place to do."[11]

---

10. Ibid., 283.

11. Ibid., 284.

The next day, at ten-thirty in the morning, the police appeared at the Basque Youth headquarters to shut it down. In the absence of the organization's highest-ranking leaders, it was Lombana himself who signed the document, although not without first adding that he "protested the closure, within the terms of the law, with the greatest possible vigor and to the extent allowed by law against such an act of force." An hour and a half later, the office of the Basque nationalist labor union, Basque Workers' Solidarity (Eusko Langileen Alkartasuna-Solidaridad de Trabajadores Vascos, ELA-STV), was closed. The inexorable effects of the uprising were already being felt.

A few days later, the rebels began taking action against individual dissidents. As one might expect, Lombana was also detained and jailed by the rebel forces. Basque nationalist activists faced the dilemma of either publicly renouncing their ideology and supporting the uprising or submitting to the reprisals and the harsh repression exercised by the insurgents. Lombana never forgot the Basque nationalists who succeeded in preserving their economic and social status by giving up their patriotic principles.[12] Lombana had not come into the world to surrender. He con-

---

12. Lombana never passed up the opportunity to make an ironic comment about the Basque nationalist activists who failed to rise to the occasion at the decisive moment of the military uprising. Even in the report included in the appendix, he alluded to someone by the name of Ibarbarriaga who acted as a guard while he was in prison, about whom he recalled that he was a "minion of the Araba Provincial Council and former Basque nationalist." In 1937, however, with memories still fresh, he defended a more rigorous view. He maintained that "the rich man has taken the side that he believes will win, and the poor man has remained loyal." The list of examples is not to be missed: "Generally, the men of abundant economic means, and despite the bond payments in insurgent territory, took the side of the rebellion, in the belief that they could better defend their interests that way. Ibarrondo (Don Manuel), to keep his position as secretary of the Caja de Ahorros Municipal [Municipal Savings Bank], has written numerous letters expressing allegiance to the rebel movement. Trocóniz (Don Pablo) did the same. Odón Langarica, id. Echauri (the Carlist Requeté treasurer of the Basque Youth), id. Jorge Urquijo (Gorka), director of the Urquijo Bank, id. Mués, editor-in-chief of *Euzkadi in Araba*, went to Somosierra as a volunteer, like Carlos Hernández (a nationalist), who despite being forty years old, was a volunteer on the Bergara front. Ángel Fajardo, one of the first [Basque] nationalists in Vitoria-Gasteiz, in order to keep his position with the Bank of Vitoria, deferred to the movement. Kepa Arcaute, employed by Bajo and a leader of the Mendigoxales [a Basque nationalist youth movement centered around hiking], joined the Hermandad Alavesa [Brotherhood of Araba], reporting to them about the internal affairs of the [Basque] Nationalist Party. Luis Aramburu and Emilio Cuevas also collaborated with the militia. Venancio del Val, editor of *Euzkadi in Araba*, joined the Falange, writing in opposition to the Basque nationalists. Gregorio Lascurain, employed by Casa Orbea [a well-known local company], joined the militia and the Red Cross, in order to keep his positions. José María Ortiz de Mendivil, an agronomist, who shortly before the outbreak of the movement had been studying the agricultural part of the Basque Statute with another specialist, Mr. Irazusta, out of fear of losing his position and in order to defend his interests, is a staffer for the Provincial Council and parades through the streets with his red beret . . .

tinued unreservedly professing the same fervent allegiance to the Basque national cause that he had been declaring for years, and the radical coherence of his activist behavior ended up landing him in prison. The insurgents reacted energetically and intransigently to the slightest indication of resistance; Lombana was detained and immediately jailed. He entered the Vitoria-Gasteiz jail on August 1, 1936, beginning, as we will see, a pilgrimage through various penitentiaries that would last until mid-1937.

Lombana after two months in the temporary prison housed in the convents of the Carmelitas Descalzos in Vitoria-Gasteiz. Source: José Luis de Abaitua.

The testimony quoted above was given by Lombana a year after the events recounted, still soon enough so as not to have radically distorted his memory. The account is highly detailed and plausible. Furthermore, it is confirmed by a similar account given by Javier de Landaburu of what happened in Vitoria-Gasteiz during the days immediately following Franco's uprising, and specifically, the role Lombana played in his party's initial actions.

Don Valentín Santamaría, a member of the EAJ-PNV's National Justice Tribunal, joined the factionalists in the belief that with them, his Jesuit son, who was in Marneffe, could return to Spain." See José Miguel de Barandiaran, *La guerra civil en Euzkadi*, 286. On the other hand, he could duly appreciate the Aguirre y Basterra brothers of Vitoria-Gasteiz, about whom he affirmed, in 1976, that they "are admirable, [although] they've got Julián, the one who was in jail with me, a bit isolated and almost kidnapped, and he's the one who's worth the most," Letter from Lombana to Irujo, Bogotá, December 24, 1976; Archivo Iñaki Anasagasti, Fondo Lombana. On the harsh terms in which Lombana censured those in the former group, see the discussion by de Pablo, who points out the inaccuracy of some of his information and notes that "the analysis of the list of nationalists who changed sides . . . does not reveal this dichotomy between rich and poor," *En tierra de nadie*, 258.

In the account given to Father Barandiaran, Lombana remained humble concerning his actions, aspiring to paint a portrait of himself that his fellow party members could endorse in all details. On the evening of July 18, 1936, Landaburu recalled, "don José Luis de la Lombana called me from the Basque Youth, telling me to come to that center. I did so. There Lombana told me that, through information that had been confided to him, he knew that the military was going to rise up, declaring a state of war early the following morning." The former parliamentary representative ratified Lombana's account of the decision adopted by those gathered at the Basque Youth premises: "we agreed," he noted, "those of us who were in the Basque Youth (not the EAJ-PNV), to be in contact with the republicans in order to prevent the uprising from breaking out in Vitoria-Gasteiz. Lombana and [*sic*] went to be with the republicans at their circle."[13]

Lombana, far left, in prison in Vitoria-Gasteiz.

As one of the Basque nationalist activists detained[14] by the insurgents in Vitoria-Gasteiz in the days following the uprising, Lombana endured

---

13. Barandiaran, *La guerra civil en Euzkadi*, 311.

14. He used to explain that according to the official version, he went to jail for just one reason: a line in a column that he wrote for the newspaper referring to the newly appointed mayor of Vitoria-Gasteiz as "the gallant baker and eloquent military man," something which constituted an intolerable insult to authority.

Lombana, seated center, next to man with cape and beret, during his time in the prison in Vitoria-Gasteiz.

the suffering and unpleasant incidents that accompanied being held as a political prisoner. He was sent first to the provincial prison and subsequently to the Carmen jail in Vitoria-Gasteiz. He learned firsthand about the cruel treatment of detainees and prisoners, the interminable interrogations, threaded with insults, derogatory remarks, and abuse, the simulated executions, and the savage practice of "excursions" (*paseos*) that the insurgent forces used with the most prominent prisoners, executing them in a ditch or clearing in the woods and abandoning their corpses on the side of the road.[15] For Lombana the experience was very hard, inhuman beyond question. In his report, Lombana recalled "those who were shot among the prisoners in Vitoria before I got out of jail numbered eighty. Adding those who were executed without being imprisoned first and those who were murdered after a longer or shorter period of house arrest or of imprison-

---

15. He would later recall that while he was in jail, a German officer asked to see him. He could not have been more surprised, since he had no idea who he was. The German asked him whether he remembered him, and when he said no, he explained that he was the man who, during the La Blanca fiesta of Vitoria-Gasteiz two years earlier, as part of the street attractions, cut out paper silhouettes in exchange for a few coins, and that he had made silhouettes for him and the friends who were with him. At that time, he told him, he was already doing intelligence work. God knows, Lombana used to say, what the officer really wanted, because after telling him this, he took his leave, and he never saw him again or heard anything more about him.

ment in houses of detention other than the ones I was in, the total comes to somewhere between one hundred and fifty and two hundred. This is as far as Vitoria is concerned."[16]

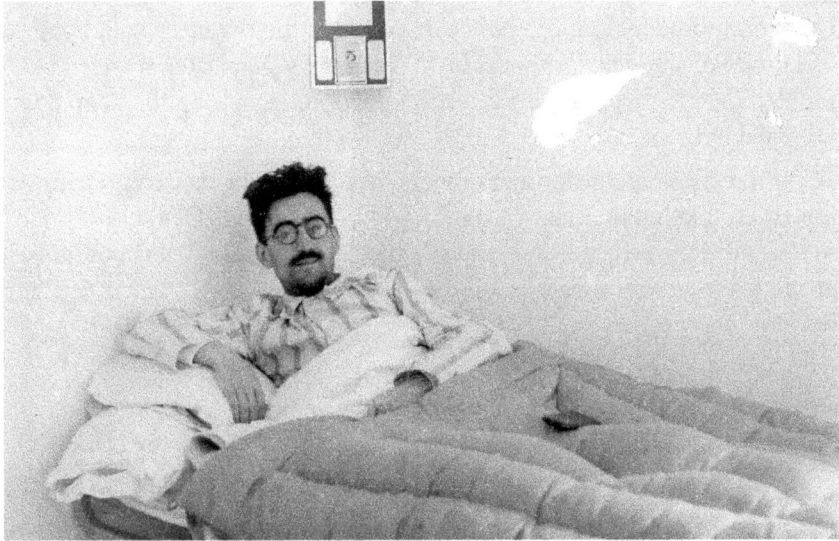

While in prison, Lombana contracted bronchial pneumonia.

In the winter of 1936, Lombana became ill with bronchial pneumonia. The terrible living conditions in the prison, lack of warm clothes, unhygienic facilities, and scarcity of food, seriously undermined Lombana's health, leaving him in a state of collapse. He was only able to recover thanks to the care of his cellmates.[17] Despite everything, Lombana never lost his good humor.[18] This intelligent man never descended from the elevated, and hence relativist, perspective from which he analyzed and evaluated the occurrences of daily life.

---

16. Barandiaran, *La guerra civil en Euzkadi,* 294.

17. When he recovered from his illness, he quit smoking, something that, he used to remark with a laugh, was another example of the regime's therapeutic advances.

18. On the most visible wall of his cell, he wrote this maxim: "Here, the one who doesn't kill himself to adjust will die from the adjustment" ("*Aquí el que no se aclimata se 'aclimuere'*"). On one occasion, a group of prisoners came to him to propose a hunger strike, because their ration was twenty-two garbanzo beans. His response: "What kind of a strike are we going to declare, if 'they' have already done it for us?" When the electricity in Bilbao was cut off, a soldier shouted to him, as he was standing in the patio along with the other prisoners, "Lombana, they have no lights in Bilbao," to which he responded, "Good, that way they'll fight in the dark." General laughter followed, and punishment for Lombana.

A restless man with great initiative, Lombana constantly attempted to escape, eventually slipping out of prison, catching his jailers unprepared. Once free, he headed for France, following a mountainous route that allowed him to keep his distance from the most trafficked roads, which were monitored by Franco's police. He crossed the Pyrenees with the help of a group of smugglers, who, as he told the story years later, traveled barefoot by night to reconnoiter the terrain, carrying people on their shoulders wrapped in blankets.

After crossing the border Lombana headed to Angelu (Anglet), immediately contacting the cell that the EAJ-PNV had established in Iparralde[19] to look after the refugees and organize the resistance. Lombana put himself at the disposal of the party authorities, who were not slow to assign him his first mission.

Lombana Moves to Barcelona

As soon as the insurgent army occupied the entire Basque territory, the EAJ-PNV's highest executive body, headquartered in Villa Endara in the municipality of Angelu, considered the suitability of acquiring an organizational structure in Barcelona.[20] Their interest in setting up a party delegation in the Catalan capital was not a whim of the *burukides* (party leaders), but a response to necessity. The number of Basque refugees in Catalonia was large and growing, and the precarious conditions in which the majority of them were living made it increasingly urgent to launch a system of social assistance and humanitarian support. The EAJ-PNV, which enjoyed a large presence among the Basque refugees who had sought safety in Barcelona, could not evade the responsibility to help.

The deterioration of the refugees' living conditions in Catalonia was alarming, a fact that provoked rejoicing in the Falangist media, which lost no time elaborating on the propaganda messages depicting a loyalist zone dominated by barbarism and uninhabitable for civilized human beings. For example, in late 1937 the Falangist Basque press expressed delight that EAJ-PNV leaders Manuel Irujo and Jose Antonio Aguirre had failed in their attempt to demand better treatment from the republican authorities

---

19. In Euskara, the French Basque Country or the continental Basque Country is the part of the Basque Country under the jurisdiction of the French state.

20. See Gregorio Arrien and Iñaki Goiogana, *El primer exilio de los vascos: Cataluña, 1936–1939* (Barcelona: Fundación Ramón Trias Fargas, 2002). For Lombana's time in Barcelona we have fundamentally relied on the information published in this work.

for the citizens of Basque origin who, having fled their homeland, were residing within their jurisdiction. According to *El Pueblo Vasco*, Aguirre's statements to the international press, designed to prick the conscience of the entire civilized world regarding the desperate situation of the Basque refugees, indicated "the really crushing pessimism that has hold of him," a pessimism based on the conviction that "his situation is unsustainable, since he has two great enemies in the Red zone: the Red committee and the refugees themselves, who are demanding that he demand from the former more humane treatment than what they are receiving."[21]

Clearly, it did not require many arguments to justify an active and ongoing presence of the EAJ-PNV in Barcelona. The delicate situation of many compatriots with regard to their living conditions constituted a decisive reason. The idea progressively took shape among the *jeltzale* (EAJ-PNV member) leaders, and in September 1937, the EBB (the EAJ-PNV's top executive body) formally agreed to create a delegation in Catalonia, entrusting the selection of party activists to be responsible for its organization and launch to deputy (*diputado*, elected representative) José María Lasarte.

Lombana's identity card identifying him as an official director and foreign correspondent of the EAJ-PNV.

---

21. *El Pueblo Vasco*, December 30, 1937. "Irujo and Aguirre make several pleas that are unanimously rejected. They ask for assistance for the Basque refugees in Catalonia, Valencia, and Madrid. They cannot improve their status."

Pressed by the urgency of the situation, Lasarte completed his mission in a few days. By October 9, Lasarte brought before the party executives the individuals proposed for the complicated task of establishing a foothold in Barcelona. Among them was Lombana, who, despite his youth—he was twenty-seven years old at the time—had already proven himself as a firm and committed *abertzale* ("patriot") and as a man with the capacity to react effectively in the face of adversity. Years later, Antonio de Gamarra declared,

> [Lombana] was sent to Barcelona for his great merit, for his ability to confront difficulties. When the PNV's activity began after the dictatorship of Primo de Rivera, Lombana was going about making noise. At the beginning of the war in 1936, he made his way from Madrid to Vitoria and from Vitoria to Bayonne, without help from anyone.[22]

The EBB pressed Lombana to go to Catalonia "as soon as possible," charging him with the task of writing a detailed report on the situation in Catalonia, with the goal of drawing up "some concrete instructions on the actions to be pursued by the delegation."

Lombana immediately set to work. On October 6, he wrote to his friend Javier de Landaburu, expressing his state of mind since taking on the task assigned him by the EBB:

> I'm ready to go to Barcelona. What am I going to do? I know the military danger I'm running, but even if it's significant, this does not disturb me, since I'm used to it. What I need is a diplomatic passport. I have to eat!
>
> It may be that God will allow them to keep beating up on me in this life, and one day you'll get an SOS from the City of the Counts to get me out of there. Don't forget me between now and then. I'll keep you updated on everything having to do with this.[23]

The Spanish embassy in Paris denied his request for a diplomatic passport, and his efforts to obtain one through Irujo also failed. He would have to travel under more precarious conditions than he had originally wished.

In the absence of diplomatic credentials, he succeeded in obtaining a passport on October 9 from the Spanish consulate in Baiona. The passport, valid for one year, allowed him to travel to Spain, by way of Catalonia and France. Two days later, the Baiona subprefecture granted him a visa to

---

22. Arrien and Iñaki Goiogana, *El primer exilio de los vascos*, 200n290.

23. Archivo del Nacionalismo, Li AU 9-1, R-527/5-1.

travel to Spain. Lombana entered Spain on October 15, 1937, by way of the Puigcerdá border crossing.

Five days before his departure, Lombana wrote a new missive to Landaburu, detailing his personal considerations:

> I'm going to Barcelona without a diplomatic passport. They aren't giving me anything more than a credential as the party's delegate there. I only have a consular passport, since the embassy in Paris has refused diplomatic ones. We'll see whether Irujo wants to help me get one in Valencia. On my account, it doesn't matter, since we only die once in this life. What I'm worried about is that they won't let me return, even if the party authorizes me to do so, in the event that I have to do something in Baiona on behalf of my brothers-in-law.
>
> I don't want them to believe that fear has the better of me in doing my duty. Of course, our mission is—so far—a bloodless one. Lasarte has not come, and I'll meet him in the City of the Counts.
>
> I'm leaving for Barcelona, if nothing unexpected happens, on Tuesday the twelfth, at night.[24]

The group of activists chosen to staff the mission lived up to the party's high expectations. By late October, the Basque nationalist delegation was already established in the Catalan capital. Its highest administrative body, made up of the activists listed below, included Lombana as the member in charge of political affairs:

> President: José María de Garate
> Press and Propaganda: Manuel Sainz de Taramona
> Politics: José Luis de la Lombana
> War: Juan José de Basterra
> Social Assistance: Julio de Salgado and José Etxaniz
> Social Secretariat: Marcos de Arana

On November 21, the party's premises in Barcelona were inaugurated. Following the common practice of the time, the premises were shared with the ELA-STV labor union and Emakume Abertzale Batza (the EAJ-PNV's women's section). During the following months, the EAJ-PNV Executive Council in Barcelona, also known as the Basque nationalist Delegation and Extraterritorial Committee, underwent more than one change in its membership. Lombana was one of the few members to serve without interruption. Once more, his tenacity, constancy, and firmness made themselves

---

24. Letter from Lombana to Landaburu, Archivo del Nacionalismo, LiAU 9-1 R-527/5-1.

evident as he fulfilled his commitments. He acted as the council's secretary until midyear, when the preparations began for his trip to New York to participate in the Second World Youth Congress for Peace.

What stands out from Lombana's time in Barcelona, however, is above all the fact that he was also occupied with the leadership of the daily *Euzkadi,* the EAJ-PNV's official newspaper that, withdrawn from the market following the evacuation of Bilbao in June 1937, reappeared in Barcelona at the beginning of December of that same year. Disheartened and dispersed after the occupation of their territory by Franco's army, the Basque nationalist community needed its own printed media that could report on the evolution of the civil war from a national perspective and contribute to maintaining the patriotic flame among the evacuees. Barcelona offered a sufficient infrastructure and social base to make it possible to resume publication of a paper that for years had served as a vehicle of communication among party activists and the leadership. The financial sacrifice entailed was significant. The publishing enterprise would feel the effects of this sacrifice, but to the promoters of the newspaper it seemed necessary to provide for "the continued life of the only Bilbao and Basque newspaper that can support the work of the (Basque) government."[25]

Lombana, seated on bumper of car.

The task of launching the newspaper was taken on and personally carried out by Lombana. On December 2, 1937, in accordance with the

---

25. Report to the president of the government of Euskadi, requesting a monthly stipend for the economic support of the daily. Barcelona, February 24, 1938 (Iñaki Anasagasti Archive, Lombana File).

press law, he submitted a request to the Head of Central Services of the Interior and Social Assistance Department to begin publication of *Euzkadi* in Barcelona. *Euzkadi,* the official mouthpiece of the Basque Nationalist Party, would be directed by Lombana himself. Four days later Lombana declared that the newspaper would be a morning paper, that its editorial and administrative headquarters would be located at number 589 Calle de Cortes Catalanas on the main floor,[26] and that the paper would be printed at numbers 11 and 13 Calle de Barbará, owned by La Publicitat.

On December 9, 1937, Telesforo de Monzón, minister for the interior in the Basque government, issued the identification card that accredited Lombana's status as the official director of the daily *Euzkadi* in Barcelona and as a press correspondent abroad. A work certificate issued on January 17, 1938, by *Euzkadi*'s administrator testified that Lombana was already working for the nationalist paper's publishing house. In his role as director of *Euzkadi,* Lombana not only acted as the paper's official representative, both in Spain and abroad, but also succeeded in expanding the provision of information about the Basque political situation of the time, using not only printed media, but radio lectures.[27]

It is interesting to note that the reappearance of the Basque nationalist daily in Barcelona provoked curious reactions in Bilbao. *El Correo Español,* founded after the occupation of Bilbao, was the daily newspaper of the Falange Española Tradicionalista y de las Juntas de Ofensiva Nacional Sindicalista (FE y de las JONS, Traditionalist Spanish Phalanx of the Assemblies of the National Syndicalist Offensive), or Falange for short. Once Bilbao had been won for Franco's cause, the conquerors flung themselves voraciously into the most shameless plundering of the property of the defeated. *El Correo Español* claimed the building that, until the city's occupation by the insurgents, had been used by the Basque nationalists to publish *Euzkadi.* It is unsurprising, then, that *El Correo Español* should pay a certain amount of attention to the fate of the newspaper whose presses it had come to occupy, with no better right than that of conquest. One day, the Falange's Bilbao daily printed some notes about rumors coming from the other side of the front, remarking that "Other soldiers who have also made their way clandestinely to our lines . . . have told us other things

---

26. In May, the editorial headquarters moved to no. 116 Calle Lauria.

27. The text that served him as a guide in speaking about the Basque Statute and economic harmonization and about the Basque Statute and the integration of our institutions stems from one of these cycles.

about life in Barcelona, such as, for example . . . the upcoming appearance of the Bilbao daily *Euzkadi* in the capital of Catalonia."

The Bilbao paper did not restrict itself to simply reporting the rumor; it presented the news with a notably mocking tone. It may have amused *El Correo Español* writers and administrators to occupy the press by force of arms, causing *Euzkadi* to try to carve out a place for itself in the daily newspaper market using another's buildings and presses, located in another city. The article's headline anticipated, between defiance and sarcasm, the upcoming reappearance of *Euzkadi* in the Catalan capital. The jeering title read: "On how *El Correo Español* is left without a press: Because Aguirre is going to publish *Euzkadi* in Barcelona."

In fact, *Euzkadi* did resume publication in Barcelona, not on its original press, which remained in the hands of *El Correo Español* for many years, but on that of another publication. Its first director was José Luis de la Lombana, who held that post until July 30, 1938.

During the period in which he led *Euzkadi*, Lombana promoted many initiatives. Shortly after *Euzkadi* began to publish, Lombana requested a monthly subsidy of twenty-five thousand pesetas from the Basque government's propaganda budget. Lombana did not demand measures of positive discrimination in favor of *Euzkadi*.[28] Aid of this kind was also granted to other periodicals that published official information from the Basque government, providing their readers with news of Aguirre's cabinet's activities.

The twenty-five thousand pesetas requested did not even cover what the paper would have made if it had charged the usual advertising rates for the articles and reports that the paper published about the Basque executive. The newspaper's leadership noted that it was, de facto, "the Basque government's sole mouthpiece," since the official declarations and announcements of the autonomous territory's executive "and the details and reports that are of interest to the different departments" were published in *Euzkadi* every day. In addition, *Euzkadi* carried out an enormous amount of propaganda work in favor of the Basque national entity. The text of the request to the Basque government specified that in the "editorials and articles" its staff composed, "the work carried out by the Euzkadi government" was defended on a daily basis, "in many cases putting the

---

28. Report to the president of the government of Euskadi, requesting a monthly stipend for the economic support of the daily. Barcelona, February 24, 1938 (Iñaki Anasagasti Archive, Lombana File).

Lombana, seated front left, with other members of the EAJ in Barecelona, c. 1937.

lie to false reports published by other dailies or publicly stated by parties opposed to the mentioned work." Only thanks to the publication of *Euzkadi* was it possible in Catalonia to find out about "the Basque government's work, which would otherwise have been unknown," or worse, been discredited by false reports.

In addition, the daily also carried out a less prosaic mission. Its publication had "formed and strengthened the spiritual ties that should exist among the Basques residing in territory loyal to the Republic," and thanks to its appearance, the Basque evacuees had been given "guidance in accordance with the spirit of Euzkadi." Those in charge of the paper were persuaded that if "the morale of the Basques resident in France" had been maintained, it was thanks to the reading of *Euzkadi,* the redaction of which had "prevented the decay that was already beginning to be noticeable among those patriots." Additionally, copies were daily sent abroad, "chiefly to the Americas and France," indicating that the nationalist newspaper was an excellent "propaganda vehicle in favor of our cause."

There was another initiative worth noting that originated with *Euzkadi.* Around May, Lombana drew up a questionnaire on the economic aspects of the Basque government's actions since the government's formation. He sent the questionnaire to Pedro de Basaldua, Aguirre's private secretary; Javier de Landaburu; and the minister for justice and culture, Jesús María de Leizaola.[29]

Lombana, who was trained as an economist and a historian, was conscious of the significance that systematic data collection could have in acquiring complete and trustworthy information about the economic policy designed by Aguirre's executive branch during the conflict. For this reason, he tried to convince his comrades of the need to pay special attention to this point, "in order to bequeath to those who will govern Euzkadi tomorrow the experience we acquire in this social convulsion." He thus pressed them to respond to his questionnaire: "studied today, with data, [the economic phenomena of the war] can be of great use tomorrow."

The highly comprehensive questionnaire included eleven points covering all aspects of the government's economic policy, from monetary issues to the private property regime by way of the financial system, prices, reforms in business administration, and the collection of funds to finance the costs of the war. We do not know whether Lombana obtained the replies he sought, although we can say that, in the event of their existence, they would constitute excellent material for acquiring first-hand knowledge of the economic aspects of the public activities of Aguirre's government.

During his stay in Barcelona, Lombana also participated in various efforts aimed at promoting the exchange of specific prisoners whom he knew personally. From the correspondence he maintained with the secretariat of Manuel Irujo and José Giral, it can be deduced that he was interested in an exchange of prisoners: an infantry captain from Vitoria-Gasteiz named Miguel Anitua, who was a prisoner in Burgos, for the artillery captain Carlos Magaz, who was held in Montjuich. He also worked to promote the exchange of Manuel Ibarrondo Vidal-Abarca.

Lombana Embarks for the United States to Participate in the Second World Youth Congress for Peace and Returns to Donibane Lohizune

The trip referred to in Lombana's unpublished report took place between August and November 1938. Lombana's journey to New York will be

---

29. Documents by Lombana, addressed to Basaldua and Leizaola, dated in Barcelona, May 17, 1938 (Archivo Iñaki Anasagasti, Fondo Lombana); the copy sent to Landaburu in Archivo del Nacionalismo LiAu 9-1 R-455/4-8.

examined in more detail later, in the chapters dedicated to discussing the circumstances leading up to the report and its contents. We merely note for now that, after the end of his tour, Lombana did not return to Barcelona because in late 1938 the wartime situation made it seem that Barcelona would not remain under republican control much longer. It was not long afterward that Franco's army began the final offensive that carried the front line to the Spanish-French border. Lombana saw that his mission in the Catalan capital had come to an end. His only possible refuge was French territory.

On October 26, 1938, he was still in New York. He wrote to Landaburu in Paris, informing him that "I will leave for there on the fifth. I am embarking on the *Paris,* and I will arrive over there on the twelfth. Then," he added, "I will go where you send me."[30]

On November 3, 1938, the French consul-general in the United States issued him a tourist visa, authorizing him to travel to France, where he disembarked on November 18.

Once in Europe, he took up residence in Donibane Lohizune (Saint-Jean-de-Luz), confronting the disagreeable incidents and difficulties experienced by evacuees from the civil war during the final phase of the Spanish conflict. From there, he traveled frequently to Baiona and on rare occasions to Paris, evading the controls the French authorities used to restrict the movements of Spanish exiles in their territory. His correspondence from this period demonstrates that he even had plans for trips to Belgium, stopping in Paris along the way.[31]

In his travels, he had a full agenda of political contacts and meetings. His commitment to the Basque national cause meant that he continued to be active in the EAJ-PNV. The outlook, however, was not promising. The political scene was growing more somber by the day, and his personal situation was becoming increasingly complicated and unstable. It was impossible for him to cross the Franco-Spanish border; his papers were not in order, and he was known to and wanted by Franco's police. On the other hand, he also could not continue to live in France, which was becoming increasingly suspicious of the exiles from the civil war. There was no future

---

30. Letter from Lombana to Landaburu, New York, October 26, 1938 (Archivo del Nacionalismo, LiAU 9-1 R-451/6-1).

31. In a letter to Landaburu dated February 25, 1939, he informed him that "I will be going there [to Paris] on the way to Belgium, and we'll chat" (Archivo del Nacionalismo, LiAu 9-1; A161/1-6).

in France, at least not for anyone who, like Lombana, lacked income and resources to live in comfort. The atmosphere of Europe was likewise not propitious to democrats and anti-Franco resisters. Fascism was flourishing, and Europe was crisscrossed by energetic and expansive authoritarian regimes. No one knew what form events would take, but the signs were not exactly positive.

With regard to Lombana's political expectations amid this somber scene, his observation sent to Landaburu from Donibane Lohizune in late February 1939, can serve as a summary: "Not much news. It seems to me that the most that Franco, damn him, will give will be a kind of indult, such we can already say goodbye to autonomy, until the Spaniards get tired of being fascists."[32]

Like many other Basques expelled from their homeland by the civil conflict, Lombana began to look to the other side of the Atlantic, seriously considering the possibility of taking up residence in the Americas.

Lombana had friends in exile in Mexico, and he contacted them about the possibility of moving to join them. He obtained a positive response; his contacts were receptive, generously offering to host him in their homes. Colombia appeared as a second option because his brother-in-law lived there, and that family connection might help facilitate the bureaucratic steps necessary to permit the move. In addition, relocating in Columbia would be less worrisome for his family, to whom he would not appear so alone and unprotected. Finally, all these reasons led him to decide in favor of Colombia.[33]

Lombana Settles in Colombia

Once he had made the decision to cross the Atlantic, Lombana began getting his papers in order. Without having proper documents, and in the midst of being persecuted, any attempt to travel to the Americas was simply futile. He was issued a passport by the Spanish consulate in Hendaia (Hendaye), still under the jurisdiction of the Second Republic, on February 2, 1939, valid until February 24, 1941, but he did not set sail immediately. In part due to the need to conclude some pending commitments in France and in part due to the difficulty of finding a ship for the trip, he remained in French territory until early the following year.

----

32. Ibid.

33. He used to laugh when he recalled that at the time, he had felt that it was not a good idea to travel to a country like Mexico that had so recently been through a revolution.

Lombana, seated third from left, with friends prior to 1940.

On December 8, 1939, with the war now definitively lost, the Colombian consulate-general in Bordeaux stamped the previously issued passport. Three days earlier, the consulate of the Dominican Republic had authorized him to travel to Ciudad Trujillo, in transit to Colombia. Finally, on January 22, 1940—almost a year after he obtained his passport—the Baiona prefecture granted Lombana a five-day visa to depart for Colombia from the port of Le Havre. On February 3, 1940, the Le Havre subprefecture authorized him to embark for Colombia. Lombana sailed on February 6, 1940. The voyage lasted three weeks. He arrived in the port of Barranquilla (Colombia) on February 26 of the same year, on the steamer *San Diego*.[34]

His first days in Colombia were difficult. Homesickness overwhelmed him, as he indicated in a letter sent to the *burukide* Luis de Arregui: "I'm in these lands, but my thoughts are with you; at all hours, one repeats the question, 'What will they be doing ...?' We are following your struggle with something more than emotion, and we hope for victory soon."[35] Goaded by this fierce longing for Euskadi and his *jelkide* comrades, Lombana asked them to send him "spiritual fodder, pamphlets, everything that you publish, so that I don't lose my good Basque sense and so that I can continually live through all your activities. Some photos of Sabino [Arana, the founder of Basque nationalism] would come in handy."

---

34. As he told the story later, the passengers had to paint and repaint the ship during the voyage, as the flag was changed in order to avoid problems on the trip.

35. Letter from Lombana to Arregui, Bogotá, May 27, 1940 (Archivo del Nacionalismo, PNV 362-6).

Lombana did not find Columbia attractive. His remarks in his first letters about Colombia, its people, customs, and expectations, were not very positive. In the missive to Arregui that we have just quoted, he included the following reflections:

> The climate in Bogotá, which is cold, suits me. The only thing is that staying here is unpleasant for many reasons, and of course, it's very difficult to work without having any money; and I suppose that someone who had money wouldn't come here either, unless he were a fool . . . This country has no possibilities for anything without money; the people live at the expense of the government, which distributes benefices to its friends, and then they devote themselves to going to cafés more than in Seville.

In another letter addressed to Elias de Etxeberria, he described the following scene:

> [Here in Colombia] the whole world lives on what we called 'connections' [*enchufe*] over there; there's no administrative career, and the officials are the friends of the ministers; there are several patriots who enjoy that luck: Abrisketa, Perea, etc. Those of us who don't have political influence live by our wits; in the end ... God will provide . . . This country is the Spanish inheritance. The people still use phrases that bring to mind the spirit of the militia and of colonialism: 'At your orders': over there, only in the barracks did anyone conclude that way. There is no wealth, or they don't exploit it, and of course, they know that the Basques exist because there was an attempt at emigration, led by a man from Guernica [Gernika] named Seijo who, when he found out the location to which they were sending him, I suppose they wanted to finish off the race . . . You already know, if you wish someone ill, send him to Colombia, and . . . end of story!"[36]

Lombana registered with the authorities on August 5, 1940, and again on October 10, 1940. On March 17, 1941, he obtained authorization from the Colombian National Police, Foreigners Section, to remain in Colombian territory for an indefinite period.

Once in Colombia, Lombana had to completely remake his life. Despite his youth, the experience of such a change in his surroundings forced him to rethink many things: family, friends, relationships, profession, and so on.

---

36. Letter from Lombana to Elías Echeberria, Bogotá, May 27, 1940 (Archivo del Nacionalismo, PNV 326-6).

Lombana, walking on right, in Bogotá, Colombia.

Initially, he dedicated himself to agriculture. A paradox of exile: a lawyer who had studied the humanities and economics turned farmer. Lombana believed that Franco's regime would soon fall and that it was not worth the trouble to take on ambitious professional projects that would require him to remain in the Americas for an extended period. He was truly confident that he would not be absent from the Basque Country for too long. He established himself in the department of Tolima, where he was initiated into cotton growing by a farmer of Basque origin by the name of Larrauri. Subsequently, he worked for the Curtidos América company in the city of Mosquera, owned by another Basque, Andrés Perea Gallegan, who was later named the Basque government's delegate in Colombia.

However, he soon found employment, that while unfulfilling, was more in accord with his education. With his habitual sincerity, he confessed to Luis Arregui,

> Everyone is in the habit of telling grand tales when writing over there; I say this because there is a difference between what happened with Irazusta, for example, and what is known over there. I'll be sincere with you: this is frankly bad, without money and without initiatives. I'm giving some classes at the Xavierian University, to see if I can make myself known, and needless to say, the pay for the classes is ridiculous. I'm teaching 'Journalistic Technique' at the Journalism School.[37]

37. Letter from Lombana to Arregui, Bogotá, May 27, 1940 (Archivo del Nacionalismo, PNV 362–6).

In very similar terms, he informed Elías Etxeberria that "I'm giving some classes that pay next to nothing, but since there's nothing else, one must endure it. I wrote to Juanito Olazabal to look for something for me in Venezuelan territory, and he answered saying that he couldn't do anything. We'll see soon enough whether things change."[38]

With the goal of providing a more solid documentary basis for his classes on "Journalistic Technique" and to make them more rigorous, Lombana asked his Basque friends for help. He planned to write a textbook on the subject, which he was going to publish in Chile, and begged Pablo Azkue to write "a few pages on the management organization of a modern daily newspaper," adding, "If Pantaleón would like to offer some ideas, or Pikabea, Ulibarri, etc., it would come as a great help, but it seems to me that they won't do anything for the poor castaway Lombana."[39] So it was. Lombana put out an SOS that went unanswered. No one did anything for the "poor castaway Lombana," because all his fellow political activists had suffered a shipwreck similar to his own. Only a month later, Pablo de Azkue answered his request for help with a laconic note, sent from Biarritz, in which he told him

> Your letter comes at a time of real distress. Arredondo, Arregi, Andrés, Eli, and Koldo are in Gurs. Don Carlos, Don Javier, Monzón, Lasarte, etc., in a northern department.[40]
>
> Although I would like to send you the information you ask for with regard to newspaper administration, subscriptions, advertisements, propaganda, etc., and I would be happy to do so, I do not have the necessary peace of mind, nor do I have access to reference books. The good library I used to have remained behind, and I didn't bring a single book that mentions these subjects. So, I would have to make an effort for which I do not have the strength, since I also lack health.[41]

This harsh reality was puncturing his initial expectations. Shortly after the end of World War II, Lombana began to realize that the help the inter-

38. Letter from Lombana to Elías Echeberria, Bogotá, May 27, 1940 (Archivo del Nacionalismo, PNV 326–6).

39. Letter from Lombana to Arregui, Bogotá, May 27, 1940 (Archivo del Nacionalismo, PNV 362–6).

40. Gurs was a concentration camp. Department refers to the French administrative divisions.

41. Letter from Azkua to Lombana, Biarritz, June 12, 1940 (Archivo del Nacionalismo, PNV 362–6).

national community would offer the Spanish democrats to overthrow Franco's regime would not be as intense, committed, and effective as it needed to be. The beginning of the Cold War in the late 1940s put a definitive end to the most optimistic observers' expectations. It was ever more evident that, far from overthrowing Franco, the Western powers would support him, trusting that Franco's rabid anticommunism would safeguard Southern Europe from Marxist pressure. Perceptive and realistic, Lombana took stock of the situation and began to formalize his legal situation in Colombia with a view toward long-term residence. Those were times of desperation and disenchantment in the exiled Basque community. The American hope was vanishing; the assistance and support provided to the Allies during World War II had been futile. The Western democracies failed in their commitment of solidarity with the peoples deprived of liberty, and in the face of this desertion, many Basques cooled their enthusiasm for large ideals and devoted themselves to finding resolution for their small personal tragedies.

As far as his career was concerned, Lombana continued teaching at the National University of Colombia, moving from journalism to law. Soon, he turned to practicing law, his true passion. He opened his own office and combined work as a legal advisor with that of an accountant. He had to start from scratch, setting up his office in his own home.

Initially, he dedicated himself to civil law, specializing in property and family cases. Over the years, he expanded the scope of his professional activities, offering comprehensive assistance in legal and financial matters. Without abandoning his civil law practice, he began to expand into commercial and tax law, where he could demonstrate his skill with numbers. He also developed his expertise in canon law, more in order to aid the religious orders that requested his services—most often with connections in his beloved native Vitoria-Gasteiz or through the recommendation of others with such connections—than for his own profit. In the course of time, he built an excellent reputation as a serious, disciplined, and trustworthy professional. Later on, he added to his traditional occupations that of consultant and advisor, serving both individuals and corporations. When legal consultancy appeared on the country's professional horizon as a new way to avoid lawsuits, Lombana had been offering legal consultation for a long time, acting as an advisor to many prominent figures and to domestic and foreign companies.

Several times, he was on the point of being named to directorships for which Colombian nationality was a requirement, and just as many times, he was asked to make the gesture of acquiring Colombian nationality. He always refused, not out of disdain for Colombia, but rather out of respect. He felt that it was unfair to take a job away from a native Columbian when the country had welcomed him so warmly. His professional colleagues and fellow lawyers always felt that Lombana lent luster to the profession.

Likewise, in his personal life Lombana decided to stop living provisionally. He resolved to marry by proxy, because the military dictatorship installed in Spain at the end of the civil war denied him authorization to freely return to his native land. On December 7, 1946, he married María Jesús Bilbao Bastarrechea, a native of Algorta (Bizkaia) and active in Emakume Abertzale Batza. Lombana had met her in Barcelona during his months of residence there. The marriage ceremony took place in Bilbao, by proxy in accordance with canon law, while Franco's police mobilized in the area with the aim of taking advantage of Lombana's possible presence on Basque soil to detain him and subject him to the "Christian" repressive legislation that the regime applied to dissidents. Following the ceremony, the bride traveled to Columbia, arriving in 1947. The couple had two children: Miren and José Luis. The family residence was at Carrera 8, number 69–41, in Bogotá. Jose Vicente Katarain, the president of the Colombian capital's Basque House, recently passed by the location and described it as "a beautiful old house from the 1940s, European in architecture, with the Lombana family coat of arms still there in stone on its façade, even if the house no longer belongs to the family."

Lombana's integration into Colombian society did not occur without problems and difficulties. Social interactions in Colombia were conducted with delicacy and respect. Following the Latin American style, most locals were distinguished by their smooth manners—a permanent smile, measured speech, and a warm tone of voice—and by their painstaking formal friendliness. In this context, Lombana's typical Basque direct, vehement, and sincere style resulted in an initial personality conflict. This was gradually overcome thanks to the affection the locals developed toward him, due chiefly to his upstanding character and his frankness. The initial impression of Lombana as a choleric and ill-humored man that he would occasionally produce when first meeting someone was immediately overcome by a feeling of warmth and trust. The real Lombana was revealed to be a man cut from a single cloth, sincere and honorable without limit, a friend to his friends, endowed with a sharp sense of humor and with a large heart that made him ever ready to help his neighbor.

Into his old age, Lombana retained his characteristic manner of expressing his opinions: drastically, sweepingly, and categorically. Throughout his life he also practiced a very peculiar austerity, reflected in his refusal to wear evening dress or accept membership in social clubs, in the belief that such signs of luxury were unfitting for an exile. He always maintained that the country that took him in had given him enough in the simple fact of receiving him, and for that reason, he never wanted to accept public awards, recognitions, or honors that, in his opinion, should be reserved for Columbian nationals. He was a battle-hardened and upright man of profound convictions, who stood out for his directness and frankness. Decisive and clear-eyed, he was never inclined to "shades of gray." As a result of his character, he won true devotion among his friends, who professed an unconditional attachment to him because they considered him a trustworthy person and an excellent counselor, but he aroused profound hatred among those who considered themselves his enemies and envy among the inept, as often happens to talented individuals.

Like the great majority of Basque exiles from the civil war, Lombana made colossal efforts to endure his inner exile by focusing on his work. However, he could not escape the effects of an intense emotional pressure that led him to brood for long years on a profound feeling of homesickness and powerlessness. In 1959, he wanted to travel to Euskadi. Spain's General Security Directorate authorized the visit, but warned that he would be closely monitored by an agent.

Lombana's longing for his native land led him to cling to the friends of his youth, with whom he maintained an intense correspondence. He always missed Vitoria-Gasteiz and Araba, frequently recalling festivals, social events, and places of meeting and recreation. Over a long period, Lombana maintained correspondence with Manuel Irujo, among others. The contents of a number of letters they exchanged, deposited in the Basque Library of the University of Nevada, Reno, allows us to follow the long-standing, sincere, and fruitful relationship between the two.

In the first of their letters, dated 1965, Irujo replied to Lombana's request (made from Colombia) for Irujo to go through the libraries of José Antonio Aguirre and Landaburu to determine whether they still had some books on historical topics that he had given to them years earlier. The effort had been successful. The widow of the Lehendakari (the Basque president) discovered, among the books that Aguirre left behind in his library at his death, five works on historical topics whose first pages were marked with

Lombana's name and seal.[42] Landaburu, by contrast, affirmed that he did not have any of Lombana's books at his house, noting that there might be some in Biarritz, in Baiona, at Sota's house, or in Beyris. Lombana likely maintained relations with Aguirre and Landaburu in the context of the research that the two of them were engaged in with a view toward completing a history of Euskadi from a Basque nationalist perspective. Lombana, who was a historian, followed this work closely and acknowledged to Irujo years later that he had in his possession "some autograph notes by José Antonio de Aguirre, drafts for the history of the Basque Country that he was writing or thinking about writing."[43]

In Irujo's letter, references to the political situation were not lacking. Comments like those that Irujo was in the habit of making showed the disenchantment that was coming to dominate the republican generation in those years due to the evolution of events in the international political sphere. The very fact that Irujo included these comments in a letter written for another purpose is evidence that, despite the years that had passed since the war and his physical distance, Lombana followed the politics of his native land with attention and interest and was grateful for any information sent to him.

> Around here, nothing in particular. Franco continues in place. The development plan is causing inflation and is not delivering as much as was promised, but after all, it's being implemented, and many factories are being built in Vitoria-Gasteiz and all over. This is reality. Denying it does not get us anywhere. The students are protesting. Bad enemies. Elephant hunters who go to Africa have to defend themselves, in the first instance, not from the elephants, but from the mosquitos. We'll see what happens. We're organizing the Aberri Eguna [Basque national day] in Bergara, Baiona, Paris, and Itsasu [Itxassou]: the first three on Sunday are our responsibility, the fourth on Monday is Enbata's responsibility. More people are aligning themselves with the opposition to Franco every day, although they are, ordinarily, opposed to one

---

42. The books were the following: Juan Antonio Zamacola, *Historia de las Naciones Bascas* [*History of the Basque Nations*]; José Yanguas y Miranda, *Diccionario de los Fueros y Leyes de Navarra* [*Dictionary of the Fueros and Laws of Navarre*]; Tomás Otaegui, *Derecho de Gentes de Argentina* [*Argentine International Law*]; Arturo Campion, *Euskariana: Algo de historia* [*Euskariana: A Bit of History*]; *Cuaderno de Leyes de Alava* [*Book of Laws of Araba*], from 1825. The letter includes some observations about the value of the books that it is of interest to indicate here: "The book of laws, parchment, in folio, is good, it's valuable; Yanguas's dictionary is better known and widely available, but it's a good book; the one by Campión is, in my view, excellent, although I doubt that it has significant value as a book; the others are not worth much."

43. Letter from Lombana to Irujo, Bogotá, December 24, 1976.

another; but that doesn't matter: in similar situations that same phenomenon always occurs. Abroad, on the other hand, they're getting tired of putting up with us. First they were enthusiasts for our cause; then they were supporters but not enthusiasts; later they tried to get us not to present them with the bill; now they flee from us or advise us to be calm. Of course, there are exceptions, naturally, but that is what they are: exceptions. We're thick-headed enough to keep on as if the entire world were at our disposal, thinking that, if it's not, so much the worse for it.[44]

Ten years later, things had changed a great deal in Euskadi. Franco was dead, and the Basque nationalist forces were trying to stake out positions with a view toward a more than probable restoration of democracy. Lombana continued corresponding with Irujo, stating his impressions of the new situation.

His evaluation was categorical and not exactly positive. The political panorama had become notably complicated with the passage of the years. In the ideological field of Basque nationalism, leftist parties, which did not inspire excessive sympathy in Lombana, were proliferating. In this regard, it is not difficult to discern behind his words an orthodox classical liberal, convinced that it is personal effort and not the magnanimity of the state that ultimately guarantees the well-being of its citizens. His words are graphic and eloquent: "The impression given by Euzkadi today is a sad one. They all feel themselves to be patriots, even if they are communists or socialists, but this is all so that the state will give them everything they need, and they will have little to do."

The reports Lombana received from his Basque friends—his interest in the political evolution of the Basque Country remained lively until the end—spoke to him of a Euskadi very different from the one he had known. They wrote of a Euskadi in which "no one works" and that was experiencing "continual and unjustified strikes," a Euskadi in which "freedom is completely undigested."

Apart from this, Lombana was registering the effects that generational turnover had produced in Basque political life, always remaining firm in his traditional convictions and commitments. The leftist dominance of Basque politics at the time was not to his liking, and he was repelled by the self-assurance with which the young judged the role played by the previous generation, although a cynical and humorous touch was never lacking in

---

44. Letter from Irujo to Lombana, April 14, 1965.

his sagacious reflections. Nor are his views unworthy of attention regarding the Basque strategy for the defense of Euskadi within the Spanish state:

> the socialist spoiled rich kids, who do exist, tour the Americas, saying that we old folks have done nothing . . . A few days ago, some guys from Oñati [Oñate], who said that they had done so much work, were at Abrisqueta's house . . . I explained to them that in Oñati, no one has ever worked, since I understood that they were people of good taste, for example Txaquetua etc. And they wanted to do something for the PNV, which was going to the dogs . . . Everyone was silent. People are reluctant to confess that they are *jelkides*. Not me; in the face of the others' silence, I responded with what I had to say to them, and I ratified for them my old opinion, that the 'Spaniards' WILL NEVER RECOGNIZE OUR FREEDOM, whether they're Carlists or socialists. That the solution is to go and conquer Madrid, taking over the key posts through competitive examinations, etc., and so defend the [Basque] Country. All that about facilitating autonomy is an old story, and they only accept it as a lesser evil, and when the tiger has its jaws in them . . . In sum, I had to leave, and I didn't sit down to eat with them. I'm not a man for tiptoeing around, and I'm not about to change.[45]

As can be seen, Lombana felt it very strongly that anyone should be reluctant to "confess that they are *jelkides*." This was not the case for him, who considered the title a mark of glory. His loyalty to the standard was proverbial, bombproof. As he declared to Irujo in 1976,

> They sent me some papers to join with an 'application for membership in the PNV,' and I had to respond that I was still a member of the party, because I NEVER and under no circumstances had left the organization, nor had I been expelled. That it was good to renew things, but that the new and latter-day patriots could not give a green light to those of us who had ALWAYS BEEN *JELQUIDES* [sic], above and beyond the errors and intransigencies of the organization.[46]

Many years later, he viewed his youthful choice in favor of *jelkide* activism as a sign of firmness in his personal commitments: "We *jelkides* are so thick-headed that we go to the cemetery with our friends and bury ourselves with them."

His historical loyalty to the EAJ-PNV did not prevent him from having doubts regarding its future as a political organization. He believed that

---

45. Letter from Lombana to Irujo, November 2, 1976 (Archivo Iñaki Anasagasti, Fondo Lombana).

46. Ibid.

it was necessary to act realistically, in view of the dynamism and drive that leftist Basque forces appeared to be exhibiting. It was a sign of the times. Everywhere, the opinion was proliferating that the EAJ-PNV's historical cycle had come to an end and that the future leading party would be the leftist Basque nationalist forces, whose young activists were going to set the course for the future of Basque politics. Lombana's fears centered not so much on the harm that could be caused by socialism, "since work has never frightened me; I've always worked," but on "communism and anarchism in Euzkadi."

The passage of the years did not cause him to break ties with his comrades from Vitoria-Gasteiz. In the late 1970s, he was still close to his old friends and companions from Vitoria-Gasteiz, with whom he maintained a correspondence in which they exchanged political reflections. In 1976, he confessed to Irujo his concern about "their lack of political vision," saying of them that "they sing a great deal, but they don't come down to earth." His perspective was very pragmatic, and he fled from essentialism. He tried to persuade his friends from Vitoria-Gasteiz that it was indispensable to reach

> a consensus with our neighbors the "Spaniards," so that we can become members of a Europe based on nationalities. That we have no legions to defend our borders. That up to now, geographical isolation could be our element of defense—the Catacombs of Callixtus, for sure—but that now that geography and the means of communication have been overcome, it's necessary that we not be absent again from another Pact of San Sebastián.[47]

At the age of sixty-five, Lombana continued to work as a lawyer, but not without problems. "I continue practicing my profession," he confessed to Irujo in 1976. "I like it; I love it as if it were my final beloved. I earn enough to live on, and when something extraordinary comes up, an appeal to the high court, for example, for which you can charge a lot, I have to devote it to paying the clients who had deposited their securities with me, and last year my house was broken into at night, and more than thirty thousand dollars of them were taken."

At the same time, his intellectual interests remained intact. He continued to be drawn to books, which he characterized as "exile's only friends." His reflection on the role they played in his life is not to be missed: "When

---

47. Letter from Lombana to Irujo, Bogotá, December 24, 1976 (Archivo Iñaki Anasagasti, Fondo Lombana).

the tone of conversation at home changes, as a consequence of the idiots that the years have turned my wife and me into, I shut myself up in my library and forget everything. They are my second life." His main pastime was reading, followed by music. A homebody, he liked to eat well and preferred to do so at home, where, he said, his tastes were known better than anywhere else.

Lombana's fondness for books reached such an extreme that he obsessed over the protection of his library. We have already seen that in 1965, he asked Irujo to search Aguirre's and Landaburu's libraries for the purpose of determining whether they included any books that belonged to him, and if so, to return them immediately. Around Christmas of 1976, he described a comic episode. The day before, Lombana had received a visit from Patxi Abrisqueta. Abrisqueta had come to his home "to see 'BASQUE' things, for example, the *Apuntes de Historia General del Derecho Español, Deusto, Curso 1899–1900* [Notes on the General History of Spanish Law, Deusto, Academic Year 1899–1900], volume 2, by Daniel Irujo Urra." Lombana's precautions were worthy of a royal library: "I only let him take a look in my presence either at the *Ordenanzas de Álava* [Ordinances of Araba], 1672 edition, or the *Dictámenes* [Judgments] of Joaquín José de Landazuri, autograph, and other works that I caress every day with my glance . . . I let him look at little things, and I almost had to frisk him on the way out."[48]

The Paradox of Lombana's Life: The Destruction of His Personal Archive

In one of his letters to Manuel Irujo, Lombana effusively congratulated him for the recent publication of his memoirs, in which Irujo recounted his activity at the head of the Justice Ministry in the Basque government.[49] In his letter Lombana confessed that on delving into the contents of the work, he had experienced a strong emotional reaction: "I lived through so many things again! I relived so many memories, so many efforts, so many loves!" In addition to stimulating his memory and his affections, the work also satisfied his intellectual expectations. He confessed this in his letter: "It's

---

48. Letter from Lombana to Irujo, Bogotá, December 24, 1976 (Archivo Iñaki Anasagasti, Fondo Lombana).

49. The reference is to Manuel Irujo, *Un vasco en el Ministerio de Justicia* (Buenos Aires: Editorial Vasca Ekin, 1976), three volumes.

well done, and I liked it. The best thing of all, from the legal point of view, is the Chamber of Equity, which is the greatest legal advance."[50]

There is one point in this letter which we cannot fail to note. In evoking the difficult circumstances that the Basque nationalists of that generation had to endure in the days immediately following the military uprising in Spain in 1936, and afterward, when Franco from the south and Hitler from the north were closing in around the anti-fascist resisters who had been evacuated from their homelands, Lombana, such a friend of history, books, and the written word in general, could not but lament the fact that fear of reprisals had led so many people to burn documents and papers that might have been of great use in reconstructing the past. Lombana recalled specific and very graphic cases:

> When I read [in Irujo's memoirs] the things that Paco Velar did, the husband of the pianist Madinaveitia, and the burning of your archive, I became indignant. I remembered that fear pays no taxes. And the good old Paco-fatty, a great person and one who would never emulate Corporal Noval, who was weak in adversity, and an Amurrio businessman who always tried to avoid 'taxes': since fear does not pay them, they took the side of the Inquisition and burned everything!

The origin of the anger reflected in Lombana's letter was undoubtedly that passage in Irujo's work in which the former justice minister of the Basque government indicated the documentary sources that served as the basis for his work and expressed regret that he was unable to make use of those that were devoured by fire. "The documentation that I am publishing," don Manuel states in this passage, "is drawn from the archives of the Basque delegation in Paris. My personal archive, scrupulously organized by Francisco Velar Jaureguibeitia, became fuel for the flames in Capbreton, upon the entry of the German troops in 1940. It had been placed in metal boxes and buried. Its guardians judged it safer to dig it up and burn it."[51]

During that time, Lombana had experienced his own personal drama. He found himself forced to do without materials that he had tried to preserve, but that were burned out of fear of the reprisals that might be suffered by those responsible for their guardianship. Lombana wrote,

---

50. Letter from Lombana to Irujo, Bogotá, December 24, 1976 (Archivo Iñaki Anasagasti, Fondo Lombana).

51. Manuel Irujo, *Un vasco en el Ministerio de Justicia*, 7–8.

> Don't be upset. On a smaller scale, I had a suitcase with notes for the histori-
> cal record, but good old Sebastián San Vicente and Velar also delivered it to
> the flames when the Germans were approaching Baiona. . . . I manage using
> my memory, which still works, but there was material there for many books;
> I saved three, which are typed on that bad paper we had in Barcelona.

Despite Lombana's passionate and committed declaration of the need to preserve the written materials that might serve as invaluable documents for future historians, at the end of his life Lombana decided to destroy his personal archive.[52] Not out of fear of fascist violence—inconceivable now in a man of his age who had lived through such difficult situations in the course of his long life—but likely out of a more prosaic fear: the fear that haunts one who, having reached a stage at which he can look back on his life, suspects that the written traces of his existential journey will be nothing but a bothersome legacy that could not interest anyone else.

In 1976, Lombana wrote to Irujo of his satisfaction that he was able to manage "using my memory," which still remained active, but he lamented the irreversible loss of material that could have served to write "several books." His memory vanished with him, and the fatal loss of the majority of his personal documents makes it impossible for us to write the "several books" about him that his intense biography deserves. For this reason, we limit ourselves to paying tribute to Lombana with this book, which aims to recover for the Basque people the memory of an honorable, vital, passionate, deeply Basque nationalist son of Vitoria-Gasteiz who was radically committed to democracy and the freedom of the Basque people.

José Luis de la Lombana y Foncea died on October 10, 2001, at ninety years of age. His remains rest in Bogotá.

---

52. In an email that his daughter, Miren de la Lombana, sent us in July 2007 she indicated that "unfortunately," her father "destroyed almost all [the documentation] when he was already in poor health."

That Year of 1938

The report included in the appendix to this volume was composed by Lombana in 1938 and describes his activities during the trip he took to the United States that year. In this chapter we include an account of the atmosphere of the time that aims to contextualize the work, echoing the chief social and political events recorded in the press that year.

Lombana's entry permit to the United States for the Second World Youth Congress.

Lombana's delegate badge for the Second World Youth Congress.

José Luis de la Lombana was twenty-seven years old when he arrived in New York to participate in the Second World Youth Congress for Peace. He came from a country mired in a war termed 'civil,' although a hypocritical international Non-Intervention Committee permitted Germany and Italy, two countries in the iron grip of fascist leaders, to provide aid to the insurgents, not only by supplying armaments and combatants, but also with military actions executed by their own troops. Before and after the bombing of Gernika (Guernica) on April 26, 1937, the Condor Legion (a Nazi German unit that served with the insurgent forces during the Spanish Civil War) dedicated itself to clearing a path for Franco's soldiers, enabling their rapid advance on the northern front. For their part, the Italian Black Arrows threw themselves wholeheartedly into ground operations. After occupying Bizkaia they took Santander and negotiated the surrender of the Basque army in Santoña, the terms of which they did not fulfill.

As a consequence of the fall of Bilbao, the Basque government established itself in Paris and Barcelona. As we have said, Lombana took on the leadership of the daily *Euzkadi*, which, for many months, found the freedom of the press in Barcelona that was denied in Basque territory.

Life Goes On: The World Waits for No Man

In the United States, specifically in Miami, the eldest son of the dethroned king Alfonso XIII of Spain died. His name was Alfonso, like his father's, and as in the case of his younger brother Gonzalo, a traffic accident ended the life of the Count of Covadonga. Alfonso was born on May 10, 1907, in Madrid, surrounded by all the pomp and circumstance to which news of royal births gives rise. He was the Prince of Asturias and the one who would provide continuity to the dynasty. However, after the fall of the Bourbon monarchy, Alfonso renounced his supposed rights of succession to the throne in 1933 in order to marry the Cuban Edelmira Sampedro, whom he later divorced. Alfonso de Borbón married another Cuban, María Rocafort, from whom he would also separate.

The car accident took place when Alfonso was leaving a nightclub, on September 6, while Lombana was in New York. Lombana almost certainly did not hear about the accident, and if he did, he surely did not consider it important. Alfonso XIII's monarchy had fallen in 1931, utterly discredited. At that time, no one thought that such a decrepit system could ever be reestablished in the Spanish state.

What Lombana probably did not know was that on January 5 of that same year, an infant had been born in Rome who was baptized with the name of Juan Carlos Victorio. Son of the Prince of Asturias, Juan de Borbón, and of Princess María de las Mercedes Borbón y Orleans, he would be the future King Juan Carlos of Spain. When José Luis de la Lombana died in Bogotá in 2000, he most certainly knew exactly who that child was whose birth had passed him by unnoticed years before.

When his son was born, don Juan de Borbón was hunting with his friends. Evidently, responsibility is an almost genetic characteristic of the Bourbons. Since the royal family was lacking in fortune, they lived in a rented apartment at number 112 Viale de Paroli, in a building owned by the famous baritone Tito Rufo. It was a modest dwelling, with an drug store and hairdresser on the ground floor.

Six days after the birth of Juan Carlos followed the death of Juan de la Cierva, a minister in the last monarchical government in Spain and the only one who had opposed Alfonso XIII's departure into exile. The last echoes of the Spanish Crown appeared to have definitively faded away.

Lombana was surely more interested in that year's winner of the Academy Award for Best Picture, *You Can't Take It with You,* directed by Frank Capra, who also won the award for Best Director. The award for Best Actor went to Spencer Tracy for *Boys Town,* and Bette Davis won the award for Best Actress for her performance in *Jezebel.*

In Spain, the scene was more somber. On January 1, in Burgos, Franco had signed a decree designating Manuel de la Falla as president of the Institute of Spain, a kind of Spanish cultural senate aimed at uniting the activities of the various academies. It was made up of full members (*académicos numerarios*) of the Academies of Language, presided over by José María Pemán, History, the Exact, Physical, and Natural Sciences, the Moral and Political Sciences, the Fine Arts, and Medicine. While Franco's supporters occupied themselves with such matters, those defeated in the war had to explain the nature of their struggle. This was the reason for making public a series of drawings titled "Galicia Mártir" (Galicia the Martyr) by Alfonso Rodríguez Castelao based on the war. The artist was a Galician writer and deputy who had worked with the nationalist Catalans and Basques organizing and giving life to the triple alliance known as Galeuzca.

Lombana was not the only anti-Franco resister who traveled to New York. The Galician leader did so as well.

The Martians Did Not Land in New York

It is probable that both Castelao and Lombana shared the intense experience undergone by many New Yorkers as a result of a radio broadcast by Orson Welles. The broadcast caused widespread terror in the city, which was led to believe that a Martian invasion was underway. This happened on October 30 of that year, when the twenty-three-year-old Welles, leading a group from the *Mercury Theatre on the Air,* took his place in front of the microphones in a New York studio of the Colombia Broadcasting System. With a group of actors, he performed a loose adaptation of H. G. Wells's novel *The War of the Worlds.* The objective was to tell a traditional story fitting the Halloween atmosphere, but the script turned out to be eerily realistic, and the broadcast turned into a case of collective hysteria.

In this work of fiction, Martians arrive on spaceships in the form of meteorites to conquer Earth. The story in itself was a fantasy, but the way in which it was presented was very convincing to hundreds of thousands of people, despite the fact that it was interrupted on three occasions to announce that it was only a work of fiction.

The clever story was broadcast to the entire country as if it were a news bulletin, beginning calmly with a weather report. Within a few minutes, the switchboards at newspapers, radio stations, and police stations were overwhelmed by the enormous number of people who were making anguished calls in search of information.

Reporter Heywood Broun wrote in the *New York World Telegram* in the aftermath, "Jitters have come home to roost. We have just gone through a laboratory demonstration of the fact that the peace of Munich hangs heavy over our heads, like a thundercloud."[1] Broun was sure that the rise of the fascist threat in Germany and Italy had affected the psychological state of the people in the United States.

Surely, neither Castelao nor Lombana, in the event that they had understood Orson Welles's accented English, would have believed a word of the story, coming as they did from a harsh reality where those shooting live ammunition were not Martians, but rather a group of Earthlings prepared to win a war with scorched-earth tactics. However, it must have been interesting to have lived through the experience, in order to gain knowledge of how easy it was to influence American public opinion.

Castelao in New York

In July, Galician leader Castelao embarked from France for the United States of America. He departed for New York on the steamer *Ile de France*. In the United States, he took part in sixty-six events as a speaker in favor of the republican cause. He also gave three lectures in Galician and held an exhibition of his drawings during the month of November.

During that time, Castelao worked especially with Galicians, although he took part in events involving the Spanish colony. The Galicians, around twenty thousand of them, constituted the most numerous group of Spanish residents in New York. They had a set of premises that were truly formidable in their location and capacity.

At that time, there was a delegation of the Basque government in New York that made periodic reports to its president, who was exiled in Paris. The delegation was made up of Manu Sota, his nephew Ramón, and Antón Irala. In November of that year, these men, together with the president of the Catalan group, J. Fontalans, met with Castelao to exchange perspectives and share a meal.

Castelao spoke frankly. He said that he was making the trip on his own account, that he was not "connected," and that if he took part in events in

---

1. Heywood Broun, editorial, *New York Daily Telegraph*, November 1, 1938. Cited in Phillip Klass, "Wells, Welles and Martians," *New York Times Book Review*, October 30, 1988, 1.

favor of the Republic and in demonstrations organized by various Spanish associations, he did so incidentally and in order to better carry out the mission he had set for himself. That mission was to reorganize the Galicians with a view toward joint action in favor of Galicia. The context should not be forgotten, since the civil war was in its last months.

While in New York, Castelao told his Basque interlocutors and the Catalan representative, he had aroused misgivings in certain sectors by speaking to the Galicians in nationalist terms. Castelao had succeeded in overcoming these misgivings, but he told them that the chief problem was the financial one. Everything that was collected, except for what came from the Basques, ended up with the Confederated Hispanic Associations (Sociedades Hispanas Confederadas). Castelao had to exercise his wits because Galicia's legal situation was not that of Euskadi and Catalonia. Galicia's autonomy statute had not been approved, and it therefore lacked "legal" status in the Republic. For this reason, Castelao had launched a secret organization in favor of Galicia, although in appearance everything continued as before. In public, Castelao collaborated loyally in favor of the Republic.

The day after that lunch, Castelao left for Cuba. He was also planning an upcoming trip to the Republic of Argentina, where he would spend a long sojourn. His Basque companions and the Catalan representative urged him to coordinate all the organizational work he was doing with the Catalan authorities and the Basque president, José Antonio de Aguirre. The Basques were doing the same thing, and they felt that if all the representative authorities came to agreement and each was well informed about the situation of the Basques, Catalans, and Galicians throughout the Americas, then when the time came to speak in Spain and to act in favor of the different peoples' claims, they would have the means to smother any contrary Falangist manifestation in the Americas, as well as a way to exert pressure.

Castelao was completely in agreement with what was said. As a Galician nationalist, he was perfectly familiar with the absurd centralist spirit that inspired the majority of the Spanish republicans, even in exile. He remarked to his companions on the distaste he had felt for the general Republican reaction when, while he was in Valencia, the news reached him of the fall of Bilbao and he was able to see for himself that "in the state bodies there, there was rejoicing at bottom," since they saw in the loss of Bilbao a failure of the Statutes and of the Basque government.

The Galician nationalist leader promised to act as a bridge to facilitate their communication with all the organizations he might create in the course of his passage through different countries. In New York, this had already been done.

They were all of the view that the exiled Galicians, due to their large number, could exercise a great deal of influence in the Americas. In addition, Castelao believed that he had a certain influence over the exiles. With time, he would come to be the man with the greatest capacity for influence. Coordination among Galicians, Catalans, and Basques promised to be a platform of great interest for directing joint action when the right time came.

That meal in New York was followed by an event at the Galician Center to say goodbye to Castelao. The Basque government's delegate, Antón Irala, attended as an invited guest and spoke a few words. Aramburu and Ramón Sota accompanied him.

Castelao left for Havana by plane, having been invited by the Galician communities in Cuba to give lectures and exhibit his drawings. Not long afterward, his album *Milicianos* (*Militiamen*) was published in New York. In Cuba, Ernest Hemingway was writing his novel *For Whom the Bell Tolls* under the influence of a war that was about to end in a crushing military victory by General Franco, aided by Hitler and Mussolini.

The Battle of the Ebro

Unfortunately for the loyalist side, the Republic was irremediably lost when Lombana arrived in New York. Its last hope was lost in mid-July 1938, when republican troops successfully forded the Ebro River. In late November, they crossed it once more in the opposite direction, pursued by Franco's soldiers. What had begun as a great victory ended in a resounding defeat in which the Republic suffered grave losses of men and materiel.

At that point, the Catalan front no longer existed. Only a few isolated contingents, remnants of Líster's, Tagüeña's, and Vega's divisions, faced Franco's soldiers as they advanced toward Barcelona. The city was almost within range of Franco's artillery. From Barcelona there fled a terrorized population all too familiar with the treatment they could expect from Franco, whose first act on setting foot in Catalonia had been to annul the statute of autonomy.

As if this were not enough, the Republic insisted on fulfilling the non-intervention agreements signed by the foreign powers. On October 26,

1938, the last members of the International Brigades (military units made up of volunteers from all over the world that fought on the republican side) left Spain. If Negrín hoped that this would cause a reaction in favor of his administration, he was mistaken.

Franco Forms his First Government, and the Republic Enters into Crisis

Franco did not wait for the end of the war before forming his first government on January 30, 1938. This government was obedient to his direction, and his brother-in-law Ramón Serrano Suñer played a fundamental role. The State Technical Committee (Junta Técnica del Estado) was thereby dissolved.

This was the first government in which civilians participated, holding purely administrative portfolios such as the treasury, education, and public works, despite the fact that the cabinet continued to be dominated by uniformed personnel. No matter what, it was always the "Generalísimo" who held the reins of power.

The Republic's dilemma was whether to surrender or resist. The Spanish socialists, led by Indalecio Prieto and Julián Besteiro, defended the option to surrender. Resistance was defended by the communists and anarchists, in addition to Prime Minister Juan Negrín himself, who had announced the "thirteen points of victory" in May, a document that was at base a disguised suit for peace. Faced with Franco's robust refusal to negotiate, the tensions between the political factions grew sharper, even as the army divided the republican zone into two.

With the Cantabrian coastal strip lost, Teruel reconquered by the insurgents, and the Aragón offensive at its height, many felt that the end of the Republic was close at hand. Minister of War Prieto—whose title was later changed to National Defense—was especially grim about the Republic's prospects.

While Prieto defended the necessity of negotiating with Franco, La Pasionaria (Dolores Ibárruri) toured the frontlines haranguing the soldiers, and the Spanish Communist Party (Partido Comunista de España, PCE) pressured Negrín to dismiss his "defeatist" minister. That dismissal took place on March 30, when Negrín himself took over the position. Interior Minister Julián Zugazagoitia, a socialist from Bilbao, also resigned, as did José Giral (State), Manuel Irujo (Justice), and Jesús Hernández Tomás (Public Education and Health). Their posts were filled by communists and socialists who followed Francisco Largo Caballero's line. Of the latter, the most distinguished was Julio Álvarez del Vayo (State), who urged closer collaboration with the Soviet Union.

The left's determination to resist to the last man—as Negrín used to say, "to resist is to conquer"—was made more complex by the fact that the central government, which had moved to Barcelona in October 1937, coexisted in the same location with the government of the Generalitat (the autonomous Catalan government). The division of responsibilities between the two governments was an unending source of conflict, which reached its boiling point following the militarization of the entire defense industry decreed by the central government on August 11. This industry was largely located in Catalonia.

The Generalitat protested, since up to that point, it had been regulating the industry's operations. The issue was resolved a few days later with the resignation of the ministers from the autonomous territories, Irujo and Jaime Ayguadé. Manuel de Irujo resigned "in solidarity with Catalonia."

While these disputes were taking place, Franco's troops continued to advance, bombarding the cities with machine-gun fire and bread rolls. The promotion of militia leaders such as Enrique Líster and "El Campesino" (Valentín González) resolved nothing. As a last resort, the Republic called to its ranks what was later named "the baby-bottle draft [*la quinta del biberón*]," enlisting thousands of young soldiers between the ages of seventeen and nineteen.

The European Democracies Fold before Hitler

On September 29, 1938, Great Britain, France, Germany, and Italy signed the Munich Agreement, with the aim of preventing a new European war by ceding the Czech region of the Sudetenland to Hitler's Reich. The Czech government did not participate in the talks and was left with no choice but humiliated acceptance of the terms.

Both Neville Chamberlain, the British prime minister, and his French counterpart, Édouard Daladier, defended the appropriateness and suitability of this agreement to the hilt. The agreement theoretically ensured peace, but it would not be worth the paper it was written on if Hitler continued to pursue his expansionist ideas.

There was a large outcry against the agreement, and the European democracies were accused of folding out of fear of the Führer, but these warnings and accusations were useless. In order to keep the peace, no sacrifice was too great, including turning a blind eye to the evident racism suffered by the Jewish population in Germany, where harassment and forced emigration were reaching more than worrisome levels.

Germany felt strong thanks to its decisive intervention in the Spanish Civil War and the annexation (Anschluss) of Austria in March 1938, which became a triumphal military parade. A month later, on April 10, in a plebiscite, a majority of Austrians ratified their country's new political situation as part of "Greater Germany."

The idea for the Munich conference came from Benito Mussolini, after Germany issued an ultimatum (expiring on October 1) to the Czech government demanding that it abandon the Sudetenland, which had a large German population. The Czechs ordered a general mobilization on September 23. Three days later, France and Great Britain did the same, but this gesture did not prevent those countries from hurrying to Munich and permitting the dismemberment of the Czech nation, which ceased to exist on October 1.

The International Brigades Leave Spain

At the close of 1938, events of appreciation for the International Brigades were held at Madrid's Monumental Theater (November 7), in Barcelona (November 15), and in Vich (December 31). Nothing was too much to bid farewell to those who had contributed to the republican cause in the Spanish Civil War. On October 26, in the thick of the Battle of the Ebro, the withdrawal announced by Negrín at the League of Nations began. Only twelve thousand remained out of all the foreigners who had come to Spain to fight for freedom and against fascism. Many of them were never able to undertake the return trip. The farewell took on an electrifying tone:

> Comrades of the International Brigades! Political reasons, reasons of state, the preservation of the same cause to which you offered your blood with such incomparable generosity: these now require some of you to return to your homelands and send others into a forced exile. You can depart with pride. You are history. You are a legend. You are a heroic example of the solidarity and universality of democracy. We will not forget you, and when the leaves return to the olive tree of peace, mixed with the laurels of the Spanish Republic's victory, return!

It was La Pasionaria who spoke before an emotional multitude that cheered and threw flowers at the members of the International Brigades, who had provided so much support to the republican cause. Her audience, together with Las Pasionaria, Negrín, and other prominent figures, had gathered in Barcelona on November 15 to say goodbye to their comrades.

The withdrawal of the International Brigades had already been discussed by the Committee for Non-Intervention in the Spanish Civil War. It had already been decided in June 1938, in fact, to send two commissions to carry out a census of their members and supervise their departure from the country. Nevertheless, Negrín, the head of the republican government, surprised everyone in mid-September with his announcement at the League of Nations in Geneva. In the thick of the Munich crisis, Negrín announced that he would withdraw the International Brigades unilaterally, in a desperate attempt to put an end to German and Italian aid to Franco.

The Battle of the Ebro was still going on when the withdrawal began on ships and trains chartered for France. Men of various nationalities (French, British, Belgian, Polish, Swedish, Swiss, American, and so on), ideologies (Marxist, communist, anarchist, socialist), and origin (including military veterans, adventurers, and unemployed workers) thus ended their intervention in a war that was in principle someone else's, but that they had experienced as their own.

The League of Nations commission, charged with supervising this abandonment of the front (fifteen officers led by a general), counted 12,673 foreigners among the republican forces.

Among all the leaders at that time, the socialist Julián Besteiro tried most tenaciously to reach an armistice between the republicans and the insurgents. He took advantage of his May 1937 trip to London for George VI's coronation to meet with Foreign Secretary Anthony Eden. At this meeting he proposed that the great powers try to mediate a settlement of the military conflict.

Although Great Britain indicated acceptance of the idea and in fact explored the possibility, the refusal of Italy, interested in a fascist victory, and Franco's refusal meant peace was impossible. The Generalísimo was afraid that leftist forces could gain the upper hand in elections following an armistice, and he knew that only military victory would ensure his triumph.

Catalonia about to Fall

Franco's troops had penetrated into Catalan territory, breaking through the republican lines in several places. After the bloody Battle of the Ebro, both sides' remaining armies were much reduced in size, but the strategic situation was more complicated for the Republic. Franco's major offensive launched on December 23, 1938, appeared likely to be definitive.

Paying no attention to the Vatican's call for a truce on the grounds of the imminence of Christmas, Franco gathered the bulk of his army to unleash his offensive against Catalonia. He did not want to let the opportunity slip past. Following the deployment of forces on November 16 on the right bank of the Ebro River, the republican troops were in a very dangerous situation. The Army of the Ebro, led by Colonel "Modesto" (Juan Guilloto León), and the Army of the East, under Juan Perea, were in disarray and badly armed. The insurgents took advantage of this fact, hammering the front in the knowledge that, once the barrier of the Ebro had been overcome, the gates of Catalonia would lie open. In addition, Franco expected to soon receive more German armaments.

In the Pyrenees, the movements of Agustín Muñoz Grandes and Rafael García Valiño succeeded in reaching the same objective. With a single maneuver, the republican lines along the Segre River had been pierced.

Backed by the element of surprise, Franco's most significant card was his numerical superiority. He had three hundred thousand men, supported by almost six hundred pieces of artillery, as well as five hundred planes. Facing this deployment, Modesto's and Perea's men, also numbering around three hundred thousand and coordinated by the republican army's commander-in-chief in Catalonia, Juan Hernández Sarabia, had fewer than four hundred pieces of artillery and two hundred tanks and armored cars, the majority obsolete or in poor condition. In the skies, they had fewer than eighty planes piloted by inexperienced soldiers.

The president of the republican government, who was also its defense minister, Juan Negrín, had arranged the visit of one of his men to Moscow to obtain arms, but the operation came too late. The shortage of ammunition was accompanied by the troops' low morale, undermined by the recent and resounding failures and by the severe winter that made the already difficult conditions even harsher. This was the situation at the time that José Luis Lombana was embarking for his return to Europe after his American travels. He could no longer return to Barcelona because the Basque government's delegation was already preparing to leave.

By the end of 1938, Franco's regime had been recognized by the Vatican, Turkey, and Japan. In addition, the first "Day of the Crusade" was held in November; this "celebration" was due to Cardinal Primate Gomá, who also organized the collective letter in support of Franco's cause that will be discussed in the next chapter. Finally, the emerging regime decided to restore the yoke and arrows to its coat of arms, the symbol of the Catholic Monarchs, while prisoners continued to be executed and the drums of war began to sound throughout Europe.

3

The Civil War beyond the Battlefield: The Propaganda Fight to Win International Public Opinion

Following the formation of the Basque government in October 1936, the executive led by Aguirre, with the firm support of the EAJ-PNV itself and the effective backing of several significant figures on the international scene with a capacity for influence in the Catholic world, launched a propaganda campaign. The campaign's goal was to inform world public opinion about the reasons why a largely Catholic people, like the Basques, had taken a position in the civil war on the side of the Republic and against Franco's army, an army that, at least nominally, purported to be the vanguard of a crusade in defense of Christian principles.

As anyone with a basic understanding of Euskadi in the 1930s might comprehend, the propaganda campaign was based on a distinctly simplified conceptual framework. Not all Basques were Catholics, nor did all Basque Catholics support Aguirre's government, nor were all Basques who supported the executive constituted in Gernika on October 6, 1936, practicing Catholics. At a moment, however, when public-relations portraits were being painted with a broad brush throughout the developed world—the claim that an army made up in part of North Africans that shot Catholic priests was waging a crusade in favor of the cause of Christ was not a simplification, but rather an absurdity—there was not much room for nuance. Only a clear and striking image could have an impact. Only simple, easily grasped messages were effective as propaganda.

Aguirre's initiative, however, was not a unique and original idea of the Basque government. It was not even a novel proposal among the supporters of the Republic. From its very beginning, the Spanish Civil War was accompanied by a ferocious propaganda struggle through which the contending parties sought to gain the upper hand in international public opinion, as well as on the battlefield. This was not only a fight aimed at winning favor in foreign ministries and sympathy among the shapers of opinion. In addition to a moral triumph on the stage of public opinion, the public-relations battle also pursued a more practical objective. It aspired to arouse world solidarity, with the goal of enabling the contenders to receive as much help and support as possible, in the hypothetical case that the evolution of the armed conflict turned out to be unfavorable to their interests. In the case of the Basque government, this financial aid turned out to be especially necessary in order to respond to the humanitarian demand generated by the thousands of evacuees and refugees produced by the conflict.

As the Spanish ecclesiastical hierarchy increasingly took positions favorable to Franco—an inclination that reached its height with the publication of the Spanish episcopate's collective letter of July 1, 1937—the Basque campaign also acquired growing intensity. It was not the same thing to influence international public opinion when facing an evidently anti-democratic barracks uprising as it was when facing a belligerent party that had the explicit endorsement of the country's episcopate. Subsequent to that moment, certainly a crucial incident in the ebb and flow of the opposing sides' public relations, the propaganda battle tended to focus ever more openly on the motives of the EAJ-PNV and its leaders. Despite their confessional convictions, they allied themselves, once the conflict began, with the leftist and republican forces that made up the Popular Front coalition instead of with the theoretical defenders of Christian civilization.

Practically from its foundation, the EAJ-PNV's motto had been *Jaungoikua eta Lagi zarra* (God and the old laws, meaning the *fueros*). The two basic components of EAJ-PNV's ideological foundation were the Catholic faith—at the start of the conflict already heavily colored by the strong social element arising from the doctrines of Leo XIII and their subsequent developments—and what we could generically call the political self-government of the Basque Country. The problem, then, for the party was that the civil war represented a clash between two sides whose programs split apart the pairing on which the EAJ-PNV's ideology was based.

The insurgents proclaimed their defense of the faith and the Church, tying it indissolubly to a unitary and uniform conception of Spain. This was radically incompatible with the least recognition of the political protagonism of the Basque Country and its right to freely govern its own destiny.[1]

---

1. As Hilari Raguer points out with his habitual mastery, it cannot be affirmed that the defense of the Church was what initially bound together the plotters of July 18, 1936, but "the movement very soon began to take on the hue of a crusade." See *La pólvora y el incienso: La Iglesia y la Guerra Civil española (1936–1939)* (Barcelona: Península, 2001), 78.

The conception of Spain's indissoluble unity as a kind of religious dogma directly ordained by God had been acquiring a growing presence in Hispanic conservative circles during the years prior to the civil war. Nationalist claims came to be labeled as potentially subversive and revolutionary due to their opposition to the natural order established by Providence. Following the revolutionary events of October 1934 in Spain, the EAJ-PNV had to suffer more than one invective from the right that was aided by this absurd argument. With the passage of time, this aggressive discourse would come to acquire great prominence in the argumentative repertoire used by the more conservative political sectors to taunt the *jeltzales* during the war and the postwar period.

When the conflict began to take shape, the rebels—with the complaisance of some prelates of the Church—declared themselves the supreme guarantors of the first part of Sabino Arana's motto: *Jaungoikoa*. At the same time, however, they affirmed themselves the bitterest enemies of the second part of the motto: *Lagi zarra*. If not in the first moments of the war, when the religious element did not play a large role—with maybe the exception of the Basque Country due to the early intervention of the bishops of Vitoria-Gasteiz and Iruñea-Pamplona—then as the conflict continued, this dilemma was posed to the *jelkide* activists with singular harshness.

For their part, the republicans bore the stain of the fact that, at the dawn of the conflict, an implacable activity of destruction had come forth from among their number against the visible signs of the Catholic faith, the churches and the clergy. On the other hand, the republicans offered a reasonable and more than acceptable framework for the development of Basque self-government, and not merely in the form of promises. A few months after the start of the war, a Basque statute of autonomy was approved. Under this statute an executive was established with wide-ranging competencies in numerous and highly significant spheres of public activity.

The EAJ-PNV opted for republican legality, a legality that did not prevent it from expressing its Catholic confessional character and putting it into practice. This legality also enabled the party to promote ambitious social policies—supported by the *jeltzales* in harmony with the social doctrines of Pope Leo XIII—and to create a propitious environment for wide-ranging autonomy for the Basque Country. Since this option entailed the difficulty of working with openly revolutionary leftist elements, the information campaign it promoted, under the auspices of the Basque government itself, was directed toward justifying that choice with facts and arguments. The main points were clear and simple: Franco was not a crusader for the Catholic cause, but a fascist military man waging a cruel war against freedom, democracy, and social justice, following the model of Hitler and Mussolini. If he had been a crusader for God, he would not have devastated the Basque lands, which had a Catholic majority, nor would he have practiced the most implacable and inhumane methods of war, nor shot a number of Basque priests, nor allied with the most retrograde and authoritarian sectors of Spanish society and those most opposed to social justice.

The Propaganda Battle in France: The Democratic Catholic Intellectuals

In order to publicize this set of arguments as widely as possible, the Basque government sent Rafael Pikabea to Paris. He was a practiced journalist with experience in the print press who, while not a Basque nationalist activist, had shared a candidacy in Gipuzkoa (Guipúzcoa) and a seat in the Republic's parliament with deputies from the EAJ-PNV. From the Euskadi government's delegation in the French capital, Pikabea built an extensive network of relationships with some of the most influential circles of thought in Parisian society. He began to edit *Euzko Deya*, a news bulletin that gave detailed information on the evolution of the war in the Basque Country, published the chief official declarations of Aguirre's executive, and reprinted favorable opinions expressed by the international media on the Basque question and the civil war.

The success of his mission was noteworthy. In March 1937, a report on the propaganda carried out by *Euzko Deya* was made public. The publication's influence in the Catholic world was evaluated in positive terms:

> In the Catholic field, we have sought to bring together, as a support base, all the democratic and Christian social elements that might cast a sympathetic eye on the Basque people's attitude toward the Civil War. *Euzko Deya* has won the sympathy of the Catholics of the Young Republic, of the democrats with Champetier de Ribes, of the Dominican Fathers (editorials in *Sept* and *La vie intellectuelle*), of the social Catholics with Marc Sangier who edit *L'éveil du peuple* and support the Peace Home (Le Foyer de la Paix), of the Catholics with Gay and Bidault who edit *L'aube* and *La vie catholique*, of the group around *Esprit*, etc.

The report did not exaggerate. As Jean Claude Larronde has written about the print press of the neighboring republic,[2] all the Catholic sectors mentioned in the excerpt quoted above, and even some others, put their arguments, influence, and respective publications at the service of the cause defended by Aguirre's government, exercising notable influence over French and international public opinion. Among the cited media, the daily newspaper *L'aube* stands out, having, as Larronde observes, "played a role of the first order in the struggle by certain French Catholics against Falangist propaganda, which was dedicated, above all, to creating the belief in a crusade."[3]

Still more effective was the role played by France's "official" Catholic newspaper, *La Croix*, whose sympathy for Aguirre's cause and for Basque nationalism made it the true bête noire of Franco's propagandists, who missed no opportunity to denigrate the political orientation of its editorials and even the personal character of its most eminent collaborators, with wounding epithets. Nor can we forget the brilliant roster of Catholic intellectuals, such as Jacques Maritain and François Mauriac, who tenaciously resisted accepting the characterization of Franco's offensive as a crusade. Their writings, well documented and better argued, were favorable to the position of the Basque government and acquired increasing intensity over the course of 1937, drawing return fire from the Falangist media. The Falangists reacted fiercely and aggressively against all who provided intellectual and media support to Aguirre's executive, vouching for its credibility with the international media. With the exhaustiveness that characterized him, the American writer Herbert Southworth collected the documents that record a large part of this propaganda struggle.[4]

For Franco's propaganda machine, the Basque case and its international repercussions became a kind of painful ulcer in need of urgent extirpation. The more that reports spread about the situation in the Basque Country—where a Catholic president, an activist in a confessional political party, guaranteed freedom of religion in his territory and practiced the most radical humanitarianism with detainees and prisoners of war—the more difficult it was for the Falangist media to propagate in the interna-

---

2. Jean-Claude Larronde, *Exilio y Solidaridad: La Liga Internacional de Amigos de los Vascos* (Bilbao, 1998), 44ff.

3. Ibid., 55.

4. Herbert R. Southworth, *El mito de la cruzada de Franco* (Paris: Ruedo Ibérico, 1963), 99ff.

tional media the story that the Generalísimo represented the supreme guarantee of Western civilization, fighting against the excesses and enormous dangers of communist revolution.

In their version of the war, the rebel press officers sold the image of a president (Aguirre) and a political party (the EAJ-PNV) that, swayed by ambition, had betrayed their Catholic convictions to place themselves at the service of a destructive communist revolution promoted by Moscow. A clear example of the kind of messages they issued is seen in the following teletype sent by Franco's wartime government based in Salamanca to the news agencies and communications media in late January 1937. It insists on the complete subordination of Aguirre's government to political and strategic guidelines laid down by the Kremlin.

> The Republic of Euzkadi has been turned over to Tomanov, the Kremlin's Minister in Bilbao . . . Euzkadi has risen up as an independent canton. It has its government, its bureaucracy, and the separatist dream seems to be a reality, but the nationalists are not in command, not Aguirre, nor Monzón, nor Leizaola, nor Heliodoro de la Torre. Euzkadi is mortgaged to Russia, and Russia is in command. Tomanov is the true president of the Basque government, and there is no other authority than his . . . Tomanov, a prominent figure close to Aguirre, is a Russian, in the guise of a technician, who monitors all his movements, giving him orders, even against the nationalists themselves, some of whom have already been jailed . . . The day that Aguirre wants to act on his own account, his power will end, and the Russian representative will fall on him, and with Aguirre, the independence of Euzkadi will disappear.[5]

Messages of this kind, which so clearly distorted reality, conflicted with the reports coming out of the Basque Country every day and with the statements that Aguirre's government was occupied in publicizing to the world. Moreover, if the latter could rely on the cover provided by the French democratic Catholic intellectuals for what was usually known as "the Basque cause," it was evident that the Falangist crusade myth faced an additional difficulty in its desire to penetrate the major international media.

If anyone thought that the military occupation of Euskadi would put an end to the Basque government's propaganda efforts and to the international support it received, they were quite mistaken. Following the invasion of the Basque Country by Franco's troops, Aguirre's cabinet continued

---

5. "Dificultades en el Gobierno Vasco," *La Nación de Buenos Aires,* January 30, 1937.

Lombana, seated on ground far left, with Lehendakari Leizaola.

its propaganda work in Europe and the Americas, arousing the wrath of the Falangist press, which pitilessly attacked the nationalists' determination to defend their positions on the stage of European public opinion. For example, *El Pueblo Vasco* of Bilbao missed no opportunity to criticize the proclamations periodically issued by the Basque government-in-exile to call European and world attention to the Basque case and obtain its recognition, support, and solidarity. In a January 1938 editorial, the daily struck out at Aguirre's executive, noting:

> [The] comic and tragic government that was suffered here has not resigned itself to death, and continues wandering off there somewhere, without a territory of its own, calling itself the 'government of Euzkadi.' The sheer fact of being a government with nothing to govern is already in itself highly absurd, but the fact that this bunch that had this poor land going hungry and on a regimen of crimes should announce over there that when it returns, it will reestablish normality here: that's something that more than deserves a trip to the insane asylum.[6]

This is only one example of the tone acquired by the invectives with which the Franco regime's Basque press tried to neutralize domestically the

6. *El Pueblo Vasco,* January 18, 1938.

effects of the propaganda with which Aguirre's executive presented itself and declared its aims.

Likewise, when information reached Bilbao about the radio broadcasts that the Basque government was planning to make from Barcelona in Basque, *El Pueblo Vasco* once again took up its furious diatribes against the *jeltzales,* Aguirre, and his government, using the worst epithets to denigrate the role they played during the war.

> The Basque separatists, who continue plotting with the Reds, have begun to make some broadcasts in Basque on the Barcelona radio. The poor Basque language has to support on its millennial shoulders all the stupidities and falsehoods that it occurs to them to load onto it, those repugnant wretches who would have filled these provinces with opprobrium if other men born in them had not preserved them with the dignity of their lives, and with the sacrifice of those lives in many cases . . . in its long centuries of existence, the Basque language will never have served for such ruinous ends as those to which it is being put by those dimwits who use it to satisfy their repugnant passions. The old and venerable tongue becomes merchandise on the infantilized and degenerate lips of the separatists. Now they are selling it for the low price of some bureaucratic posts at Radio Barcelona.[7]

The interest in the Basque language expressed by *El Pueblo Vasco* is curious. It had never dedicated the least attention to it, except to ridicule its use by Basque nationalists; *El Pueblo Vasco* never published an article in Euskara, and of course, never expressed the least interest in its cultivation and encouragement. Yet *El Pueblo Vasco* could not stand the idea that Basque patriots were using it for their radio broadcasts in Barcelona.

Be that as it may, French Catholic intellectuals and Basque Catholics with Christian social tendencies supported the democratic cause in the Spanish Civil War. This commitment was sufficiently worrisome to Franco's leading supporters that the regime came to adopt particularly severe countermeasures. The collective letter that Cardinal Gomá had the Spanish prelates sign as an expression of their support for Franco was itself a consequence of the "growing irritation felt by Franco's supporters in view of the lack of enthusiasm aroused by the Crusade in Catholic circles outside Spain."[8] In the missive Gomá sent to the bishops to ask for their endorsement of the text, he acknowledged that the document had been composed

7. *El Pueblo Vasco,* January 13, 1938.

8. Southworth, *El mito,* 104.

with the aim of "repressing and counteracting the hostile opinions and propaganda that, even in a large sector of the Catholic press, have contributed to shaping an atmosphere entirely hostile to the Movement abroad." The concern, evidently, was real. The situation created in European public opinion was not as favorable to the interests of rebel propaganda as the latter would wish.

However, despite Gomá's efforts, the French Catholic press continued to publish increasingly vehement articles and commentaries favorable to Aguirre's government and critical of the religious meaning that the insurgents wanted to attribute to the Spanish Civil War. Serrano Suñer, Franco's interior minister, took advantage of the celebration by rebel troops of the first anniversary of the occupation of Bilbao to pay a personal visit to the Bizkaian capital. There, he gave a harsh and insulting speech targeting those who were so determined to deny that the Spanish Civil War had the character of a crusade. The affair was not one that could be settled with small-caliber ammunition; heavy artillery and large-caliber shells were required.

The Falangist Basque press, always submissive to the dictates of Spanish power, gave extensive coverage to Serrano's address, detailing the derogatory remarks made by the Generalísimo's brother-in-law. Both *La Gaceta del Norte* and *El Correo Español-El Pueblo Vasco* printed a transcript of the speech, including a singularly embittered reference to the French Catholic press, which had resisted the diffusion of the regime's public-relations slogans, and to some of the most eminent figures whose bylines graced its pages:

> More dangerous today than the enemy in the trenches is this other enemy who acts through politics and diplomacy, who influences our adversary in Europe ... Here and now, specifically, I want to point as examples to Maritain and to a certain press that, to our sorrow as Catholics, with tribulation in our souls, we fear to read. [Jacques] Maritain, the president of the Committee for Civil and Religious Peace in Spain. This converted Jew, who commits the infamy of launching to the four corners of the world the tale of Franco's slaughters and the immense stupidity of the legitimacy of the Barcelona government, and *La Croix* ... Is it that Maritain and his friends, [François] Mauriac and all the collaborators of that enemy press, is it that they do not know that, despite the clowning of a self-proclaimed minister of that migratory Euzkadi government, they do not know that in Spain, that in Red Spain there is no public worship?[9]

---

9. *El Correo Español-El Pueblo Vasco,* June 21, 1938; *La Gaceta del Norte,* June 21, 1938.

This speech was widely circulated in Bilbao, but it also had an immense echo in all the territories of the rebel zone.

La Gaceta del Norte mentioned the "clowning" of the "self-proclaimed minister" of the "migratory Euzkadi government" on its front page framed in red. Nothing less could have been expected at a moment when delegitimizing and discrediting Aguirre's work was one of the chief themes of rebel propaganda in the now "liberated" Basque territory.

In addition, the Bilbao press highlighted the content of the remarks in fervent editorial commentaries. *El Correo Español-El Pueblo Vasco* hammered home the points made by Serrano Suñer with a vehement and furious text titled "Todavía sobre 'La Croix'" (Still about *La Croix*), in which the irritated paper referenced its well-known French Catholic counterpart:

> It is the prototype of a kind of newspaper that would go on to establish a following all over the earth, just as, to our misfortune, certain foreign political forms would do the same.
>
> This kind of rootless, spiritually castrated, epicene Catholicism had, to our great misfortune, we repeat, an excessively verdant and baneful bloom in Spain. . .
>
> In Spain, in effect, true Catholicism has to be united, as it has always had to be intimately united, with the most heartfelt and profound love for the Fatherland, since it has been Spain's supreme aspiration from time immemorial to be the armed might of the Cause of God. This has been tragically and gloriously reaffirmed in these days in which, Serrano Suñer noted, our heroes and martyrs are dying for God and for Spain on the front lines and in the Red zone's dungeons . . .
>
> *El Correo Español,* on the other hand, as is well known, was born as the expression of a Movement for which religious and patriotic affirmation are absolutely fundamental and inseparable. For this reason, we had no need to do any violence to our inclinations when the sword of Franco and the ardently national spirit of the Movement required all Spaniards who do not want to be on the other side of the barricade to serve a Spain that is One, Great, and Free.
>
> The patriotism that today informs the entire Spanish press, thanks to the National Movement, is for us an attitude that springs spontaneously from the bottom of our souls.
>
> Being an organ of the Traditionalist Spanish Falange, as *El Correo Español* is, it is for us a natural position, and one in which we have no need to do any violence to our inclinations, to indignantly reject the iniquitous campaign of *La Croix* and to affirm that our Cause is that of God and Spain, under Franco's

command, and this with cordiality and sincerity, and without mental reservations of any kind.[10]

For its part, *La Gaceta del Norte* elevated the words of Serrano Suñer to no less a category than that of "the voice of justice and truth in response to a campaign of falsehoods." Its position was no less obsequious than that of its colleague:

> Among the subjects examined by the minister of the interior, there is one that, due to its importance, we are in a hurry to examine: we allude to a man and a newspaper, both French, that trumpet their Catholicism . . . We have the sacred duty to speak loudly and clearly, to unmask those who, owing everything to the Catholic faith they trumpet, have become tools of communism, God's enemy; complaisant vehicles, when not inventors, of the most infamous slanders, because they drag Spain's name through the mud and want to cover with spittle the sacred tombs of those who have died, their faces toward heaven, invoking Christ's Holy Name and making it their battle cry in the agony of their last moments.[11]

On that day, reporter Aureliano López Becerra applauded, "until my hands were about to fall off, the serene grace, the manly forthrightness with which Mr. Serrano Suñer judged before the world, from Bilbao . . . the miserable conduct of Spain's enemies located across our borders."[12] Could one ask for greater and more complaisant adulation? What favor would López Becerra have been expecting in exchange for proclaiming such praises of the government's leading minister?

As if all this were not enough, the following day, a new editorial in *La Gaceta del Norte* once again vilified Jacques Maritain and his "peculiar Catholicism," highlighting the fact, pointed out by the minister, that he was a "converted Jew." This was a detail that, in the author's judgment, explained "his obstinacy in the low role of a propagator of falsehoods that he has been playing, . . . his ways of understanding scholasticism, his smooth words, and the overwhelmingly pagan air of his work and his style."[13]

The battle, of course, did not end there. The French Catholic democrats and those responsible for Falangist propaganda at the highest levels would long continue launching contrary messages. This even involved

---

10. *El Correo Español-El Pueblo Vasco,* June 23, 1938.

11. *La Gaceta del Norte,* June 22, 1938.

12. Ibid.

13. *La Gaceta del Norte,* June 23, 1938.

exchanging open criticism.[14] Moreover, it also made use of categorical dis-
qualifications.[15] In sum, it resulted in a dialectical confrontation that did a
great deal of damage to the communication strategy designed by the rebel
side.[16] Evidence of this can be seen in the fact that until the end of 1938,
the Bilbao newspapers did not cease their taunts. After the civil war had
come to an end, an editorial in *ABC* espoused the view held by much of the
media close to Franco. They argued that French Catholic democratic intellectuals had influenced the opinions of many international circles about
the meaning of the Spanish civil conflict. The conservative daily accused
the "Republic of Euzkadi" (in quotation marks) of having been "one of the
most important international cards played by Red diplomacy." In its judgment, the Basque political community, led by a Catholic president and
administrator of a regime in which the churches, the clergy, and the liturgy
had enjoyed a level of respect worthy of commendation under wartime
conditions, formed an effective cover for the interests of the republican
side. They felt that it "served up to Catholics like Maritain and Mauriac, *La
Croix* and *L'aube,* the farce of the 'religious normality' of the Red zone."[17]

---

14. We might mention, as an example, an item published in *El Correo Español-El Pueblo Vasco*
on August 13, 1938, titled "No calumniamos señores de 'La Croix'" ("We are not slandering,
gentlemen of *La Croix*"), responding to the August 11 issue of *La Croix,* which made critical
mention of the "daily diatribes of *El Correo Español*." As may be imagined, the response kept
no ammunition in reserve: "We have repeatedly said that *La Croix* has placed itself on the side
of Moscow and against the Christian meaning that our war has in National Spain. And this is a
truth as large as they come, which could only be overturned with an evident demonstration that
the hammer and the sickle are not dominant in Barcelona, or by proving that it is there that the
Pope has his diplomatic representation . . . We are honored that *La Croix* distinguishes us with
its dislike. We ourselves would never know how to be friends with the Pharisee, whom Scripture
calls a 'whited sepulcher.'"

15. *El Correo Español-El Pueblo Vasco* characterized *La Croix* as a "rag in the service of the
Popular Front" and labeled its content "anti-Spanish sophistries" (see, for example, the edition
of September 14, 1938).

16. A brief list of some of the newspaper items that fed this polemic on the part of the Falangist
newspapers, following the invective launched by Serrano Suñer, includes: "Mauriac," *El Correo
Español-El Pueblo Vasco,* July 5, 1938; "Inmundicia moral," *El Correo Español-El Pueblo Vasco,*
July 6, 1938; J.F. Lequerica, "Una llaga," *El Correo Español-El Pueblo Vasco,* July 23, 1938; "No
calumniamos, señores de 'La Croix,'" *El Correo Español-El Pueblo Vasco,* August 13, 1938; Jorge
Claramunt, "Con la Acción católica y contra La Croix," *El Correo Español-El Pueblo Vasco,* August
14, 1938; editorial, *El Correo Español-El Pueblo Vasco,* October 21, 1938; "La verdad histórica y
la verdad actual," *El Correo Español-El Pueblo Vasco,* November 12, 1938; "Un equidistante con-
tumaz," *El Correo Español-El Pueblo Vasco,* December 17, 1938; editorial, *El Correo Español-El
Pueblo Vasco,* December 28, 1938; "¿Oirán los demócratas blancos esta voz autorizada?," editorial, *El Correo Español-El Pueblo Vasco,* December 31, 1938.

17. *ABC,* June 18, 1939.

Books and Movies as Propaganda Tools

The propaganda battle between the opposing sides in the civil war was not fought only on the field of the periodical press. It also appeared in books and movies. In order to defend and spread the views of the Basque government, a series of books was published during the years that the conflagration lasted. Translated books were widely distributed, providing anyone who wished to develop a deeper understanding of the causes and circumstances of the conflict with the necessary reading materials, going beyond the superficial level at which the communications media operated.

One of the first of these books was published in Bilbao, shortly before Franco's troops occupied the Bizkaian capital. Authored by Ángel de Zumeta,[18] it was titled *Un cardenal español y los católicos vascos: La conciencia cristiana ante la guerra de la península ibérica* (A Spanish Cardinal and the Basque Catholics: The Christian Conscience Faced with the War in the Iberian Peninsula). The book replied, with noteworthy dialectical effectiveness, to the open letter that Cardinal Gomá had addressed to Lehendakari Aguirre, after the latter had publicly denounced the shameful silence with which the Spanish ecclesiastical hierarchy had responded to the shooting of several Basque priests by rebel forces. The work had a major impact among Catholics. Perhaps encouraged by the success obtained by this first book, Zumeta published another work that same year in Paris. His second book was equally critical of the Spanish hierarchy and effusively favorable to the cause of the Catholic Basque nationalists. It was a second installment that went into greater detail on the arguments made in his first work. Its title eloquently reflected its subject matter: *La teología de la invasión fascista: Los documentos episcopales y los nacionalistas vascos* (The Theology of the Fascist Invasion: The Episcopal Documents and the Basque Nationalists).

Around the same time, another book was published in France that would also exercise considerable influence on European public opinion. It was originally written in French, with the evident aim of obtaining the widest possible publicity for the positions it defended; it should be remembered that at that time French was probably the chief linguistic vehicle for elite cultural communication in Europe and around the world. Written by

18. It was originally thought that the anthropologist José Miguel de Barandiaran was hiding behind this pen name. It has subsequently been maintained that the pseudonym could belong to Pantaleón Ramírez de Olano, director of the daily newspaper *Euzkadi*.

the professor Alfredo Mendizabal,[19] it bore the title *Aux origines d'une tragédie: La politique espagnole de 1923 á 1936* (At the Origins of a Tragedy: Spanish Politics from 1923 to 1936).

The work entered the publishing market with solid endorsements. The first edition, dated 1937, included a prologue by Jacques Maritain. Maritain added a polemical declaration against Franco and the crusaders that he had published a month earlier, to much controversy, in the *Nouvelle revue française*. The second edition, dated 1938, included an introductory reflection composed by the famous French author François Mauriac.

Another work with great public impact was the early work by Víctor Montserrat,[20] also published in 1937 under the title *Le drame d'un peuple incompris: La guerre au Pays Basque* (The Drama of a Misunderstood People: The War in the Basque Country). As their titles clearly reflect, all the publications addressed the question of Catholic Basque nationalism and how it confronted the dramatic dilemma caused by the Spanish Civil War.

In 1938, a pamphlet by the priest Iñaki de Azpiazu was published in Paris. With great descriptive power, he denounced many of the excesses and outrages committed by Franco's army starting in July 1936. Published under the pseudonym of Iñaki de Aberrigoyen, it bore the title *Sept mois et sept jours dans l'Espagne de Franco* (Seven Months and Seven Days in Franco's Spain). The same year saw a work "signed" by Dr. de Azpilikoeta[21] and titled *Le probléme basque vu par le cardinal Gomá et le president Aguirre* (The Basque Problem as Seen by Cardinal Gomá and President Aguirre). That same year, Iñaki de Azpiazu published a pamphlet on the same topic, under the title *El caso de los católicos vascos* (The Case of the Basque Catholics). The prologue expressed the author's aim in writing the pamphlet:

> The attitude taken by the Basque Catholics in the current Civil War in Spain has been debated and rejected by no few sectors of Catholic opinion in Europe and the Americas.
>
> The Basques are the target of a double accusation: 'The Basque Catholics,' it is said, 'have declined to unite with Spain's right wing in its struggle against communism. Moreover, they have in fact allied with the latter to combat the former.'

---

19. It is interesting to note that, despite his surname, Alfredo Mendizabal was not Basque. He was an Aragonese Christian Democrat who taught in Oviedo.

20. The pen name belonged to the Catalan priest Fr. Josep Maria Tarragó.

21. The pseudonym belonged to Lehendakari José Antonio Aguirre himself.

The two accusations are extremely serious ones, and on their basis, a fierce campaign has been waged against the Basque Catholics.

In this work, I want to take up these accusations in order to analyze them with complete impartiality, objectively, in the light of the facts.[22]

One of the works that made the greatest contribution to publicizing the uniqueness of the "Basque case" and the need to consider it independently was without a doubt the book *The Tree of Guernika*, published by British journalist George L. Steer in London in 1938. This was not an argumentative essay designed to take a polemical position, but a journalistic account, written by a war correspondent who personally experienced the northern campaign. Since Steer clearly sympathized with the Basque nationalists, his work served to spontaneously imbue its thousands of readers the enthusiasm he expressed throughout its pages for the cause of the "Catholic Basques." Steer's book was easy and pleasant to read, composed by the fluent pen of a reporter who was a master of his craft. As we will see, this work, originally written in English, turned out to be particularly useful for explaining the "Basque case" to American society.

Obviously, the rebel side was quick to engage in this propaganda battle. In 1937, José Luis Goyoaga published *Las cárceles euzkadianas* (The Prisons of Euzkadi) in Bilbao. It was a collection of articles published in *El Pueblo Vasco* that were pitiless in their criticism of the Basque nationalists. The audience was, fundamentally, Basque citizens unattached to Franco's cause, whom the author sought to attract to the rebels' views by reviling and denigrating Aguirre and his government. The same year saw the publication of a document collection that aimed to synthesize the ecclesiastical hierarchy's position regarding the conflict. Published in Burgos, the work bore a telling title: *Ha hablado la Iglesia: Documentos de Roma y del Episcopado español a propósito del Movimiento Nacional Salvador de España* (The Church Has Spoken: Documents from Rome and from the Spanish Episcopate on the Subject of the National Movement, the Savior of Spain). Its central objective was to persuade Catholics that the cause of the Church and of the faith had been defended by Franco's troops, who enjoyed the unanimous blessing of the entire ecclesiastical hierarchy.

In 1938, the publicist Rafael García de Castro wrote a book titled *La tragedia espiritual de Vizcaya* (The Spiritual Tragedy of Bizkaia). A review

---

22. Iñaki de Azpiazu, "Prólogo," *El caso de los católicos vascos* (Caracas: Ediciones Gudari, 1939).

included in the daily newspaper *ABC* (in Seville) summarized the book's objective by noting that it was offering "to Spaniards and to the world" material with which "to make a proper judgment about the strange and lamentable phenomenon of Basque nationalism." As we might suppose, the disqualification of Aguirre and his Catholicism was devastating: "Word is already going around that the Catholic Aguirre, despite his fervor and his daily Communion, has taken steps toward the threshold of Masonry, seeing the failure of his attempt to lord it over the little Basque republic, which he wanted to put beneath his feet."[23]

Following the conclusion of the conflict, the winning side mobilized its publishing firms to put out new books endorsing its position. It was a matter of crushing the side that had already been defeated militarily, with arguments to which no reply was possible. (The censors would never allow the publication of works asserting the contrary position.) Two of these apologies were published in 1939: one by the International Catholic Information Center titled *El clero y los católicos vasco separatistas y el Movimiento nacional* (The Clergy and the Basque Separatist Catholics and the National Movement) and one by Pedro Altabella titled *El catolicismo de los nacionalistas vascos* (The Catholicism of the Basque nationalists).

Likewise well-known was the book published by priest José Echeandia on *La persecución roja en el País Vasco: Estampas de martirio en los barcos y cárceles de Bilbao; Memorias de un ex cautivo* (The Red Persecution in the Basque Country: Images of Martyrdom on the Ships and in the Prisons of Bilbao; Memoirs of a Former Captive), which came off the presses in Barcelona in 1945. In the work's introduction, Javier Olondriz publicly declared the intention of instructing the reader "to what abysses of servility and to what peaks of responsibility, by complicity with the most criminal companions, the Basque separatists were lured by their unhealthy and outrageous hatred for Spain; and how with all their pretended Catholicism and their proclaimed religious fervor, despite holding power, they did not prevent the revolutionary persecution in that region, as in all the other regions of Spain, from taking on an eminently sectarian and anti-Christian character."[24]

---

23. *ABC*, December 6, 1938.

24. Javier Olondriz, "Introducción," in José Echeandia, *La persecución roja en el País Vasco: Estampas de martirio en los barcos y cárceles de Bilbao; Memorias de un ex cautivo* (Barcelona: publisher unknown, 1945).

Finally, we cannot fail to mention the book by journalist Ramón Sierra Bustamante under the title *Euzkadi: De Sabino Arana a José Antonio Aguirre; Notas para la historia del nacionalismo vasco* (Euzkadi: From Sabino Arana to José Antonio Aguirre; Notes for the History of Basque Nationalism). The author, an enthusiast of the monarchy and a ferocious opponent of Basque nationalism, confessed that the book's aim

> is the desire that those who, in Spain and abroad, have always been loyally and fervently on our side, but who have been won over by certain false aspects of the Euzkadian positions, gain a better understanding of this Basque problem. When we had occasion during the war to stroll through the cloisters of Rome or along the avenues of Saint-Jean-de-Luz [Donibane Lohizune], accompanied by good friends of National Spain, we never heard them say to us, "Poor Murcians! It's necessary to understand them!" But more than once we were told, "Poor Basques! It's necessary to understand them!"[25]

As is evident, both sides used dialectical ammunition to explain their position to an international public, and the "Basque case," which mobilized many European Catholic intellectuals in its favor, constituted a very uncomfortable topic for Franco's propagandists. They were forced to multiply their efforts and determination to publicize their position in order to prevail in influential circles.

Finally, movies also served as a vehicle for publicizing Aguirre's cause, defending his government through propaganda showings. In this area, the short 1937 film *Guernika,* produced by Nemesio Sobrevila, commissioned by the Basque delegation in Paris, and jointly financed by the Basque government and the government of the Republic, played a singularly prominent role.[26] As we will see, *Guernika* was extensively used as a communicative foundation on the basis of which to promote the perspective on the civil war defended by Lehendakari Aguirre. This was the case in Europe, and it was also the case in the Americas, including the United States.

---

25. Ramón Sierra Bustamante, *Euzkadi: De Sabino Arana a José Antonio Aguirre; Notas para la historia del nacionalismo vasco* (Madrid: Editora Nacional, 1941), 17.

26. See in this regard the excellent work by Santiago de Pablo, *Tierra sin paz: Guerra civil, cine y propaganda en el País Vasco* (Madrid: Biblioteca Nueva, 2006), 100–46.

4

The Euzkadi Government's Delegation in New York

The success obtained in France—and by extension in many other places in Europe—with the propaganda campaign promoted by the Paris delegation encouraged the Basque government to attempt similar initiatives in other latitudes. It should come as no surprise that among these countries Aguirre decided to give a preeminent place to the United States of America: a rich, powerful, and influential country, with a great capacity to condition the foreign policy of other nations and an extraordinary power to shape the international political scene.

Penetrating American society, however, was not an easy task. U.S. political culture was governed by unique parameters that could not be assimilated to those of the European democracies. Political life in the United States had very marked peculiarities, requiring methods of action that were to some extent different from those used in Europe.

In this chapter we will first describe President Roosevelt's position with regard to the Spanish Civil War and then review the attitude adopted by American society in general and the Catholic world in particular toward the armed conflict that shook the Spanish state between 1936 and 1939. All of this will serve to contextualize the work carried out by the Basque delegation that opened in New York in 1938 and, of course, Lombana's activities during his trip to America between August and November 1938.

Roosevelt and the Spanish Civil War

In order to understand the state of opinion and the policies of the American administration in relation to the Spanish Civil War, which was entering its very last stages when Lombana arrived in New York, it is necessary to realize that U.S. policy regarding the Spanish Civil War had to be coherent with the general policy the United States was pursuing with regard to the problems of Europe. On the other hand, the dominant role played in European affairs by Great Britain, France, Italy, and Germany must be stressed from the beginning. The United States acted to a significant degree in harmony and coordination with France and above all with Great Britain.

In 1935, President Roosevelt had signed a Neutrality Act that required the administration to impose an embargo on shipments of arms, ammunition, and war materiel to all warring nations. In this way, the act discriminated against countries that were the victims of aggression.

In February 1936, Congress passed a second Neutrality Act. The new act limited the scope for presidential action even further, requiring a ban on loans to the belligerents and the extension of the embargo to any nation that entered a war after it had begun. However, the act was only applicable to international wars, so the outbreak of the Spanish Civil War resulted in a special situation.

The first significant problem that American diplomacy had to confront was that of the ships that supplied fuel to Spanish warships in the port of Tangier. General Franco threatened to bomb these ships. Although the United States had not accepted Tangier's international status, and the international administration's decisions did not apply to American nationals, Secretary of State Cordell Hull ordered the consul not to support any initiatives by American nationals seeking to provide supplies to any party in the Spanish conflict. This was in line with the position unanimously adopted by the Control Commission.

On July 29, 1936, Spain's General Cabanellas sent a telegram to Washington announcing the formation and assumption of power by the new government of the Spanish state, with the title of the National Defense Committee (Comité de Defensa Nacional), provisionally headquartered in Burgos. Simultaneously, reports were coming in from the various embassies in Europe about their host governments' attitudes toward the conflict.

On August 5, Cordell Hull met with his advisors to define U.S. policy with regard to the war underway in Spain. Two days later, Under Secretary of State William Phillips sent a circular cable to all the consulates in Spain and to the embassy in Madrid, the legation in Lisbon, the diplomatic agent in Tangier, and Ambassador Claude Bowers, who was in Donibane Lohizune. In the cable, he clarified the American government's position.

The Neutrality Act, passed on August 31, 1935, which established an embargo on arms, ammunition, and war materiel, did not apply to the Spanish case, since it applied only to wars between states. The American government's policy of noninterference in the internal affairs of other countries, whether in peacetime or civil conflict, caused it to refrain from any intervention in the Spanish situation, a situation that was characterized as unfortunate.

Significantly, the term "civil war" was avoided, using the expression "civil conflict" in its place. Another term to be avoided was "neutrality"; likewise, it was considered inopportune to grant the insurgents belligerent status while continuing to recognize the Second Republic.

On August 17, 1936, the ambassador in Madrid, Claude Bowers, announced in a cable from Hendaia that the Argentine ambassador, the dean of the diplomatic corps, had organized a meeting to discuss the possibility of mediating in the civil war.

Washington's response was immediate; they clearly declared their intention not to interfere in the Spanish conflict. Under these circumstances, the ambassador was instructed to not participate in the meeting.

Almost simultaneously, the news reached Washington that the Uruguayan minister of foreign affairs had sent a communiqué to the states of the Americas suggesting mediation in the Spanish situation. The State Department's response to the Uruguayan minister was in the same spirit: the American government would scrupulously refrain from engaging in any interference in the unfortunate situation existing in Spain.

Shortly thereafter, Bowers reported once again that the Argentine ambassador had called a new meeting of the diplomatic corps to arrange an exchange of civilian prisoners. In his view, the initiative would not be accepted by the republican government, since the rebel prisoners were individuals of power and influence, and the loyalist prisoners were of scant importance. Under these circumstances, there was a risk that the diplomatic corps would be drawn into the internal dispute, a probability underlined by the partisan positions adopted by the diplomats. Twenty-four hours later, in a new cable, he reported that the diplomatic corps would also try to mediate to stop the bombing of open cities. The petition would be addressed exclusively to the republican government, which would face a negative reaction from public opinion if it refused.

Once again, Washington's response was immediate. Bowers's decision not to attend the meeting was approved, and it was left at his discretion whether or not to attend future meetings. Six days after this cable, on September 1, 1936, the secretary of state in person, alluding to the appearance of press reports on the proposals to humanize the war, reiterated to the ambassador in Spain that he was not to deviate in any way from the policy of strict non-interference. Nevertheless, they were going to try to exercise moral influence, supporting the steps that might be taken to humanize the conflict. He wished to be informed of the proposals made to Madrid and their status, with a view toward adherence or non-adherence to the joint initiatives pursued by other governments, as well as whether there were objections to making the same proposal to the rebel leaders.

The following day, Bowers cabled the text of the proposal addressed to republican minister Augusto Barcia and expressed his conviction that declining to participate had been the correct decision. Subsequently, Barcia's non-committal response and press reports misinterpreting the action and the purpose of the initiative came to confirm Bowers's caution. U.S. policy thus became more clearly defined: support for humanitarian commitments and actions, but at the same time, remaining scrupulously within the limits of non-interference in Spanish internal affairs. At the same time, the embargo on arms, ammunition, and equipment was not a legal embargo in the Spanish case, but rather a moral embargo that could be considered in large part as a demonstration of American international cooperation at a moment when the Non-Intervention Committee was trying to establish itself in Europe and hastening to act in coordination with France and Great Britain.

Roosevelt's Position

President Roosevelt was immediately informed about what was happening in Spain, by way of the embassies and through the press itself.

The U.S. ambassador to Spain, Claude G. Bowers, was a political appointee and a friend of the president. His reports, of some significance, would also be quite slanted, with notable errors during the entire civil war. Despite the scant credit he would end up obtaining at the State Department, his influence on President Roosevelt should not be underestimated.

Franklin Delano Roosevelt received Bowers's first personal letter, dated August 26 in Hendaia, in early September. In that letter, the ambassador put him on his guard in the first paragraph, noting that nine-tenths of the press reports were false. He then went into detail on the real meaning of the struggle and the underlying elements that conditioned it. In his judgment, Manuel Azaña was the one great statesman in Spain and in Europe—not mentioning the fact that he had never paid attention to the reports of a possible military coup; the conspiracy, he had been told by the Count of Romanones, had begun the day after the elections—a phrase that

Roosevelt himself underlined; the rebels were counting on a quick victory. They had relied on the navy, on the Basques, and on the assumption that the people would not rise up and fight with such great spirit.

He also indicated that the rebels had not stopped to consider that many non-commissioned officers and soldiers were not on their side, given their worker and peasant origins. In his judgment, if the rebels won, a military dictatorship with a Consultative Council would be installed. Parliamentary government would be eliminated, and constitutional guarantees would be suspended, ending the freedom of the press, freedom of speech, and the program of public schools. The Church's old privileges would be restored, the Jesuits would return, all the laws passed under Azaña's regime would be abolished, strikes would be criminalized, and the agrarian reform would be ended, expelling the small farmers and returning the lands to their previous owners. Possibly, a plebiscite would be held to restore the monarchy, despite the fact that the military was not in favor. In a word, Spain would go back to the sixteenth century. The result of this transformation would be nothing other than communism.

Another significant aspect of this letter is Bowers's high estimation of the savoir-faire of the republican leaders, even Diego Martínez Barrio, contrasting them to the right-wing leaders who had sought refuge in France and Portugal. Likewise, he contrasted the actions of the republican government to the actions of the rebels. The republican government acted in accordance with the law, scrupulously respecting the rights of the accused, and in the event that they were convicted and executed, seeing that they were given consideration and attended by priests, whereas the rebels killed without legal process. He blamed the government's enemies, chiefly anarchists and syndicalists, for the Republic's excesses. Following this comparison, he gave his personal opinion about the international situation. The possibility that the crisis would precipitate a European war was a matter of concern. Germany and Italy were openly in favor of the rebels, and France and its ambassador were openly in favor of the republican government. In his opinion, the United States should not become involved in Spanish internal affairs of any kind and should dedicate itself strictly to extracting Americans from the danger zones, looking after American interests exclusively. In a postscript to the letter, he added in his own hand that his sympathies were with the republican government, given that the rebels were the same kind of people who opposed Roosevelt's presidency.

Roosevelt, in a letter dated September 16, 1936, echoed the ambassador's opinions and noted that he was right about the distortion of news reports. The Hearst syndicate press and most conservative publishers were spreading stories of all kinds of atrocities by the "communist" government in Madrid, but they said nothing about the rebels' atrocities. He was also, Roosevelt added, correct about the need to maintain complete neutrality in Spanish internal affairs. He was happy that practically all Americans who wanted to leave Spain had succeeded in doing so; those who remained had had many opportunities to leave, and they could not do any more. The only thing that concerned him was what might happen to a consulate if a city was sacked.

As is evident, President Roosevelt was not especially concerned about the communist danger, nor did Bowers's reports highlight it. The issue of the communist danger, it must be emphasized in light of some affirmations made with a certain frequency in the public mass media, was a marginal element in the definition of American policy with respect to the Spanish Civil War.

The problems that generated concern in these first months, as Roosevelt's letter reflects, concerned the evacuation of American citizens in the face of the wave of violence that had been unleashed and the uncontrolled armed groups, as well as the protection of American property; the capital invested in businesses and stocks was estimated at $80 million.

If the policy of protecting American citizens was successful, the attempts to protect properties and businesses met notable failure in the republican zone; in the insurgent zone, by contrast, confiscation was rare. In late 1936, a significant event took place, the debate over the Embargo Act for Spain.

The Embargo Act

We previously discussed how the embargo on arms, ammunition, and equipment was not a legal embargo in the Spanish case. In August 1936 the State Department's Office of Arms and Munitions Control received a request for clarification from the Glenn L. Martin Company on what its attitude would be toward the sale of eight bombers to the Spanish government.

The response was somewhat delayed, since opinion at the State Department was quite divided. Roosevelt was not in favor of sales of this kind, since he felt that they were not in line with his administration's policy. Finally, the letter of reply stated the administration's position: non-interference in the internal affairs of other nations, and as a consequence, arms sales were not compatible with the spirit of administration policy.

The letter became public, limiting the State Department's freedom of action. Shifting from this position would create problems not only in Congress, but also in international relations with France and Great Britain. Everything seems to indicate that the possibility of lifting the embargo in light of the war's course was not considered; rather, it was assumed that the war would be brief.

On the other hand, the embargo in the Spanish case was received favorably by the press. The administration's request to refrain from selling arms was respected during the conflict's first few months, despite attempts to violate the policy indirectly, exporting small quantities by way of Mexico and France. When the government of the Republic attempted to force the situation, the matter took on a different aspect. The case that sparked the involvement of Congress was that of the president of the Vimalert Company, Robert L. Cuse, who sought to export planes, motors, and spare parts worth $2,777,000. The press, urged on by the State Department, attacked Cuse's decision.

On December 28, 1936, when the concession of the export licenses was announced, a State Department spokesman criticized Cuse's decision, calling it very unfortunate at a time when Great Britain, France, and other European powers were trying to strengthen the non-intervention accord. Roosevelt considered it legal, but not patriotic.

The case motivated a review of the U.S. position until that point. At first, Roosevelt proposed that Congress grant him discretionary authority to resolve the problems arising from an internal conflict in a foreign country. The administration tried to have new legislation rapidly passed that would bar arms exports to Spain, making Cuse's initiative futile. The matter was discussed by senators, officials, and the president himself, ultimately leading to a formula in which the issue of Spain was separated from the issue of the neutrality laws in general, and the president's discretionary authority was eliminated. In this way, the issue was treated as an emergency matter, without complicating it by introducing general legislation on neutrality, which would have given rise to a lengthy process in the two houses of Congress.

On January 5, 1937, new licenses for the export to Spain of arms and ammunition worth $4,507,000 were granted to Richard L. Dinely. This, together with the rapid loading of Cuse's shipment on the *Mar Cantábrico*, created a feeling of urgency about the need to act.

The Senate passed the resolution unanimously, and the House of Representatives did so by a vote of 411 to 1. The joint resolution took effect immediately, on January 8, 1937. By that date, the *Mar Cantábrico* had sailed for Veracruz, Mexico, to take on another arms shipment. Paradoxically, the ship would end up being intercepted by Franco's forces on March 3, 1937.

The joint resolution made illegal the export of arms, ammunition, and military equipment to Spain from anywhere in the United States, or to any third country for subsequent shipment to Spain, so long as the situation of civil conflict continued there. Licenses granted for the export of these items were canceled. When, in the president's judgment, the conditions of civil conflict had ceased to exist, he was to declare this new situation, and only then would the joint resolution cease to apply. The joint resolution had been passed almost unanimously, and it would now be difficult for the president and his administration to find room to maneuver.

Subsequently, in April, a new resolution on neutrality was debated, amending the joint resolution passed on August 31, 1935. In this resolution, the president was given authority to establish an embargo in the event of civil war in a foreign state, if the war was on such a scale or took place under such circumstances that the export of arms, ammunition, or equipment from the United States would threaten or endanger the peace of the United States. Nevertheless, the Spanish case remained outside the president's area of discretion. This was reflected in the record by a statement by Representative McReynolds.

Although Roosevelt considered the possibility of declaring an embargo against Italy and Germany due to their intervention in the Spanish Civil War, the problem was complicated. The republican government had not acknowledged the existence of a state of war with Italy and Germany, and on the other hand, reports from the ambassadors in Europe warned against action of this kind. British foreign secretary Anthony Eden said clearly that an expansion of the embargo could be considered, at best, premature. Hence, American policy did not change during 1937.

In 1938, the matter was reconsidered in light of the Austrian situation and the possibility that the insurgent forces commanded by General Franco would be victorious. This was the year that José Luis de la Lombana arrived in New York.

The policy of appeasement being pursued by Great Britain was judged negatively by President Roosevelt and the State Department, but there was great reluctance to oppose British policy and establish a dynamic in Europe that could lead to war. A feeling of Anglophobia began to take hold among some senators and representatives, and the forces favorable to the republican regime increased their pressure on the president and the State Department. They requested the lifting of the embargo in the Spanish case.

The State Department's legal advisor prepared a memorandum on this topic on March 31, 1938. The Office of Arms and Munitions Control did the same on April 11. Their conclusions were quite similar: the joint resolution of January 8, 1937, had not been annulled by the Neutrality Act of May 1, 1937. There was no indication in the debates over the latter piece of legislation that Congress had the intention of making a further decision on the Spanish issue, authorizing the president, under certain conditions, to end the embargo imposed by the joint resolution of January 8, 1937. In addition, the joint resolution of May 1, 1937, specifically stated that its purpose was to amend the joint resolution passed on August 31, 1935; therefore, it seemed logical to conclude that the joint resolution did not amend or repeal any other legislation. Perhaps for this reason, on May 2, 1938, Senator Gerald Nye introduced a resolution to eliminate the arms embargo on Spain. The situation became difficult to manage, and the sector of the press that was favorable to the republican cause began to attack the State Department and, in particular, certain officials.

Following various debates at the State Department, it became clear that the American administration could not change its policy unless France and Great Britain did so first. Hull issued a statement, and subsequently held a press conference, at which he defended his subordinates who had been attacked by the press and expressed his disapproval of Nye's resolution. President Roosevelt had left for a cruise to the Caribbean on April 30, 1938, and faced the problem on his return, on May 8. On May 9, he brought together several members of Congress at the White House and met with Hull, and a few days later he approved the draft of a statement to be sent to the Senate Foreign Relations Committee warning against lifting the embargo in the Spanish case. A change of policy under current circumstances would only add complications to a very difficult European situation.

Nevertheless, on August 31, 1938, writing to Claude Bowers, Roosevelt told him clearly:

I do wish that our British friends would see the situation as it seems to be—but as you know, they are doing everything to stall off controversy and possible war until at least 1940. It is amazing and sad to note that so many small nations have lost their confidence in England during the past two or three years.[1]

The Quadripartite Conference in Munich

One month later, the four-power conference took place in Munich. The agreement forged among Great Britain, France, Italy, and Germany meant the dismemberment of Czechoslovakia, with the annexation of the Sudetenland to Germany.

Following this meeting, France unilaterally recognized the Italian conquest of Ethiopia, on October 5, 1938, and proceeded to name an ambassador in Rome. Ten days later, ten thousand Italian volunteers departed for Naples from Cádiz. In mid-November that same year, the Anglo-Italian accord came into effect. The war appeared to have been decided. In this situation, Interior Secretary Harold Ickes wrote a letter to President Roosevelt, dated November 23, 1938. He described what had happened at a conference of lawyers held in Washington a few days earlier and the prominent role played by some Catholic lawyers. All had been of the opinion that however the Spanish Civil War might have been viewed at the beginning, the issue now was that Hitler was becoming master of Spain and would ultimately dominate Latin America. In their judgment, this constituted a threat to the Catholics of Spain and Latin America.

Another topic that had been stressed at the meeting was the fact that the arms embargo against the republican government induced doubts in Latin American governing circles. They worried about whether a government of leftist tendencies threatened by an insurrection supported by the fascist countries could count on being granted the right to purchase military equipment in the United States in order to suppress the insurrection. It seemed quite clear that Germany's and Italy's emissaries would fan the flames of these doubts at the Pan-American Conference in Lima and would use the situations created in Spain and Czechoslovakia as evidence that friendship with the totalitarian countries brought material advantages.

---

1. Dominic Tierney, *FDR and the Spanish Civil War* (Durham, NC: Duke University Press, 2007), 88-89. Quoted from Roosevelt to Claude G. Bowers, August 31, 1938, Franklin D. Roosevelt and Foreign Affairs, vol. 2.

Ickes, who was deeply familiar with the sympathies of President Roosevelt for the republican cause and knew he was a committed antifascist, was himself a supporter of lifting the embargo. He proposed to counteract this kind of propaganda by reopening the possibility that the republican government might purchase arms in the United States. This initiative would have tremendous moral effects not only in Latin America, but also in Europe. Ickes believed that French and British policy was still sufficiently fluid to be strongly influenced by the posture adopted by the American government. This was a very optimistic assessment. Ickes introduced in his letter several arguments developed in the document that the Lawyers Committee had addressed to the president. The situation had changed significantly since May 1, 1937. At that time, there seemed to be an honest effort to stop arms shipments to both parties in the conflict, through the mechanism of naval patrols by the four powers and French border controls, a mechanism that would be abandoned shortly afterward. The committee added that since the conditions that led to the imposition of the embargo had disappeared, the president had the authority to revoke it.

On November 25, 1938, the president telephoned Sumner Welles and asked him for information on this last point. Welles, after consulting Secretary Hull and legal advisors on the issue, sent the president a letter stating that the promulgation of the Neutrality Act of May 1, 1937, had not repealed the joint resolution of January 8, 1937. If the president revoked his proclamation of May 1, the ban on the export of arms, ammunition, and equipment to Spain would remain in effect. Once he had laid out this position, Welles explained to the president the possibility that the Pan-American Conference in Lima might propose mediation. In his judgment, this possibility deserved favorable consideration.

Nevertheless, three days later, in a memorandum to the attorney general, Roosevelt requested a study of the embargo on Spain. He laid out the legal situation created by the two resolutions, the State Department's opinion as presented by Sumner Welles, and the contrary opinion of the Lawyers Committee, which believed that the January 8 resolution was canceled by the resolution of May 1. While the Justice Department began to prepare a response, Sumner Welles sent the president a new document with the State Department's legal reasoning, in response to a memorandum from the president passing on Ickes's letter.

Finally, on December 5, 1938, Golden W. Sell submitted a memorandum to the attorney general on the Spanish embargo. The memorandum, ten pages long with two appendices, concluded that the State Department's opinion that the joint resolution of January 8, 1937, had not been repealed by the Neutrality Act of May 1, 1937, lacked foundation. The president was correct in believing the claim that the second resolution repealed the first. Sell laid out the political consequences of lifting the embargo through a presidential declaration: the courts would be in a difficult position, due to the belief that the embargo remained in effect by virtue of the first resolution, and Congress might be forced to repeal the first resolution and rework the second or pass new legislation on the issue.

At this stage of the civil war in December 1938, President Roosevelt was not inclined to face down pressure from Congress, which had almost unanimously approved the embargo in the Spanish case, while France and Great Britain were seeking a settlement between the moderate forces on both sides and did not want to force a European war. Nor did the Pan-American Conference meeting in Lima propose a mediation initiative, an initiative that the State Department viewed positively at the time.

On the other hand, it is difficult to predict what would have happened had the embargo been lifted, since the Republic's treasury was empty. Following the failure of British Prime Minister Neville Chamberlain's visit to Rome in January 1939, the Spanish affair was decided. The Second Republic was not worth a European war.

After World War II broke out, Eleanor Roosevelt, at a dinner with Winston Churchill, explained that, in her view, they should have done more for the republican side during the civil war. Churchill replied that he and she would have been the first to lose their heads if the republicans had won.

In this way, American policy during the Spanish Civil War did not shift from the line adopted at the beginning: absolute non-interference in Spanish internal affairs, which, in practice, meant abstaining even from participation in any mediation initiatives. President Roosevelt's position, which was clearly antifascist and favorable to the republican cause, was not sufficient to break with American isolationism in European affairs and the leadership role played by Great Britain.

American Society and American Catholicism vis-à-vis the Spanish Civil War

The physical remoteness of Spain and the disinterest with which Americans habitually approached European political events meant that U.S. society did not pay particular attention to the Spanish civil conflict. That did not mean, however, that the 1936 war went unnoticed. Rather the reverse: it was followed and analyzed by various publications, and curiously, it was the cause of polemics and clashes between different religious groups: Catholics on the one hand, a majority (but not all) of whom were close to Franco, and Protestants and Jews on the other, more favorable to the republican side.

The majority of American society took a spontaneous position in favor of the Republic. Whatever the mistakes made—or even the excesses committed—by those loyal to the Republic, the constitutional principles that governed public life in the United States, and which were deeply rooted in the population, made it impossible to look kindly on a general who had taken up arms against democratic legality and was fighting in a civil war with the political support and military assistance of Hitler and Mussolini. As long as the war lasted, opinion polls of American society systematically reported a majority favorable to the Republic and opposed to Franco. On December 31, 1938, for example, in the last stages of the Spanish Civil War, the *New York Times* published the results of a survey prepared by the American Institute of Public Opinion. According to those results, 76 percent of the population had a favorable view of the loyalists, and only 24 percent took a position in favor of Franco.

Within U.S. society, however, the Catholic community constituted a very special group, defined by a set of characteristics that should not be forgotten when attempting to evaluate the social impact of a phenomenon like the Spanish Civil War, to which one of the contending sides attributed an eminently religious character. As evidence of this singularity, consider the fact that, in the survey just mentioned, the results among Catholics were the opposite of those among the population as a whole, with 58 percent in favor of Franco and 42 percent in favor of the Republic.

By the 1930s, the Catholic community in the United States was no longer the marginalized group it had long been.[2] For many years, American Catholics had faced the stigma of being subordinate to a foreign power, the Vatican, a widespread view in U.S. society.[3] Now, however, Ameri-

---

2. Cf. Javier Tusell and Genoveva Garcia Queipo De Llano, *El catolicismo mundial y la guerra de España* (Madrid: Biblioteca de Autores Cristianos, 1993), esp. chap. 5, on which we have basically drawn in composing this section.

3. In late 1938, Ramón Sota observed that Al Smith had not become president of the United States "because the idea that a Catholic could not be a good defender of American interests was common then" and confirmed that the Catholic community "has fought against this criterion over the last ten years." Letter from Ramón Sota to Aguirre, New York, January 22, 1939, in Koldo San Sebastian, *The Basque Archives: Vascos en Estados Unidos (1938–1943)* (Donostia-San Sebastian: Txertoa, 1991), 258.

can Catholics could rely on a national organization structured around the National Catholic Welfare Conference (NCWC), headquartered in Washington, D.C., and led by Monsignor Ready[4] and William Montavon. Their capacity for social influence was significant and growing. They controlled an extensive constellation of print media and several radio broadcasters. Their reformist vocation manifested itself in the creation of several organizations dedicated to social action and the defense of workers' rights. The most notable initiative was the Catholic Worker, a social-action movement committed to the defense of the most disadvantaged.

In the political field, the Catholic community, increasingly influenced by the Church's social teachings, was drawing closer to the Democratic Party and specifically to President Roosevelt, reinforcing its influence. In the sphere of international politics, relations with pacifist communities were particularly intense.

Already in the republican period prior to the outbreak of the civil war in 1936, opinions regarding the burning of churches and convents were grouped around two poles. The more critical positions were expressed in the magazine *America,* published by the Society of Jesus. At the other extreme were the periodical *The Commonweal,* which praised the advent of the Republic, and Montavon himself, at the NCWC.

With the inevitable nuances, this antagonism remained basically unchanged for a long time. Once the war began, the Jesuits' official mouthpiece was, in general, less sympathetic to the republicans, even coming to align itself unequivocally with the rebels. The NCWC group would show greater intransigence toward Franco, although without ever endorsing the outrages committed in the loyalist zone. *America* took a belligerent tone, although in justice, it must be specified that despite its pro-Franco belligerence, it never accepted the idea that Franco's military mission was a religious crusade. *The Commonweal* was better described as neutral in tone and inclined to views that rejected both sides. It included articles of great substance, but among the contributions it published, flimsier work was also included.

Beginning in mid-1937, the discrepancies became markedly more accentuated, as happened in other countries, following the impact made on public opinion by the bombing of Gernika. The immense majority of

4. As the Basque government's delegation in New York noted, despite his protocol rank, Michael Ready was not a bishop, but rather a "canon eligible to become a bishop [*canónigo obispable*]," San Sebastián, *The Basque Archives*, 105.

U.S. society took a position against Franco and in favor of the Republic, and among those with access to the reports and propaganda that linked the event to the specific situation of the Basque Catholics, there immediately surged an intense current of sympathy and solidarity in favor of the Basque government and its president, the nationalist Aguirre. There was no unanimity among the Catholic groups, however. The magazine *America* uncritically adopted the version put out by Franco's propaganda officers: there had not been a bombing. The town had been burned by the republican troops as they fled, and the reaction of the Basque nationalists, denouncing the occurrence before international public opinion, constituted a thorough betrayal of the Catholic cause. *America's* director, Father Francis X. Talbot, who was a contributor to Franco's U.S. propaganda mouthpiece *Spain,* dismissed reports of the destruction of the chartered town with a contemptuous phrase about red propaganda.[5] The Jesuit Joseph F. Thorning used similar terms, for which he was decorated by the winning side at the end of the civil war. *The Commonweal* was somewhat more equable and diverse in its reporting of the bombing.

Another event also influenced the debate: the publication of the Spanish bishops' collective letter in July 1937. In general, it can be affirmed that up to that point the American ecclesiastical hierarchy, except for isolated cases, maintained a reasonably neutral position. It defended freedom of religion with all its strength, as was its duty, but it took good care to avoid applauding or endorsing the totalitarian impulses that inspired Franco's supporters—impulses that were, on the other hand, not always sufficiently well known to the Americans during the first months of the civil war—or elevating Franco's belligerent mission to the category of a crusade. After the approval of the collective letter, however, things changed somewhat. In September 1937, the NCWC published with full honors the Spanish episcopate's letter as well as that signed by the American prelates in response. In the latter, the U.S. hierarchy criticized religious persecution in Spain, although without identifying it with either party in the conflict, as well as making a firm profession of faith in democracy, the principles of which they associated with those of the Christian tradition.

The response of the American Catholic bishops, however, provoked an immediate reply from Protestants. In a letter signed by one hundred and

---

5. Antón Irala was not mistaken when, in a letter to the Lehendakari, he characterized Talbot as "Franco's true ambassador." Irala to Aguirre, September 18, 1938, in San Sebastian, *The Basque Archives,*194.

fifty members of the clergy and academics, they thoroughly denounced the Spanish Church, accusing it of opposing essential democratic principles, such as universal suffrage, representative government, freedom of worship, and the separation of church and state. Yet this letter also received a reply in its turn, a document signed by one hundred and seventy-five prominent American Catholics, including both individuals associated with the magazine *America* and the leaders of the NCWC themselves, Ready and Montavon. As Tusell and García Queipo de Llano indicate, "In practice, it identified with Franco's cause, but it did so in general terms, without excluding possible errors and on the basis of a portrait of his cause that he himself would have found it difficult to endorse."[6]

What is certain is that, following the American ecclesiastical hierarchy's alignment with the Spanish episcopate, the question was definitively resolved. The American Church "was on the side of the Spanish bishops and against the republican government, more than with Franco, about whom it had a very vague idea, without knowing what kind of a regime he would found, and whose political and military actions it did not defend."[7]

This was not, evidently, what the Falangist Basque press was selling in Euskadi. Determined as it was to legitimate the Generalísimo's regime however it could, it gave wide publicity to a letter sent to the Spanish prelates by eighty-two American bishops, highlighting the "persecution" of the church in Spain. *El Correo Español* likewise took advantage of some statements made by the bishop of Ohio in 1938 in order to emphatically maintain that "American Catholics are on the side of National Spain."[8]

It is undoubtedly true that the collective letter had a positive impact on Franco's cause in the United States. Later, when some of his initial supporters discovered what Franco truly represented from a political perspective, the time would come for them to throw up their hands and lament the viper they had nursed. There were those who never backed down from their initial positions, but there were also groups that, with the passage of time, ended up discovering the authentic totalitarian face of the Spanish dictator's plans. Already in late 1939, Manu Sota expressed his delight at the evolution he perceived in some sectors of American Catholicism, as the

---

6. Tusell and Garcia Queipo De Llano, *El catolicismo mundial y la guerra de España*, 337.

7. Ibid., 339.

8. *El Correo Español: El Pueblo Vasco*, August 13, 1938.

geostrategic panorama evolved toward World War II. He wrote in a report sent to Paris:

> The Americans understand Franco's posture very well, and even the Catholics themselves have stopped playing the fool. The *New World,* [Cardinal George] Mundelein's newspaper, said the other day, "From the moment that Hitler and Stalin acted fraternally, it was clear that Hitler did not go to Spain to combat the Reds." This propaganda, which the Catholics here swallowed so easily, served only to establish German air and submarine bases. These air and submarine bases are playing a very significant role in the current war and will continue to do so, since they are protected by Franco's neutrality. Even the American Catholics who have been rabid supporters of Franco are realizing Franco's intentions![9]

For this reason, even after the American Church took an official position in solidarity with the Spanish episcopate, there remained a critical group that persisted in taking a position of impartiality, close to that promoted by Maritain in France. As Tusell and García Queipo de Llano note,

> The paradox of this group is that their minority status contrasts with the reality that a good number of American Catholics, completely spontaneously, were, as we know, much closer to the Republic than to Franco, for reasons derived from the former's democratic origin and despite the religious persecution in the area controlled by the Popular Front. This was the situation of the average Catholic, however, not very well informed about Spain or interested in it, while dissident views were found among the intellectuals or the Catholic media, better informed and, above all, therefore obligated to take a reasoned and principled position regarding the events.[10]

This group was as small in numbers as it was heterogeneous in its opinions, and its statements demonstrated, generally speaking, more rejection of Franco than attachment to the Republic. The group existed, however, and it even became a matter of concern to the more conservative communities within U.S. Catholicism.

Perhaps the media outlet that most firmly maintained its defense of a neutral position with regard to the civil war was the *Catholic Worker,* not without cost to itself, since its attitude caused it to lose readers and collaborators. Very early on, it began to echo the views of French Catho-

---

9. Letter from Manu Sota to Irala, New York, November 13, 1939 (Archivo Iñaki Anasagasti, Fondo Delegación EEUU).

10. Tusell and Garcia Queipo De Llano, *El catolicismo mundial y la guerra de España,* 344.

lic intellectuals, and it coherently and tenaciously defended peace, justice, and the Church's social teachings. Its position can be summarized in the idea that civil war was the worst evil that could befall a country and that Christianity could not allow itself to become linked with either side. More influential and with a greater circulation, *The Commonweal* observed the proprieties more carefully. Until the end of the civil war, it continued to provide a diverse platform for the expression of opinions of all kinds about the Spanish conflict. However, for the purposes of this study, it is interesting to highlight the fact that, beginning in mid-1938, it began gradually tilting in favor of impartiality, with very considered positions and very balanced reasons.

It is impossible to understand the impact of the civil war in the United States, however, without taking into consideration the neutralist context that dominated the country. Neutrality, legally mandated in American society at that time, notably conditioned the positions taken by U.S. Catholic communities in relation to the civil war. Since 1935, Americans had provided themselves with a set of laws and regulations that guaranteed that the country's hands would be tied in the face of any international military conflict. The option for neutrality was an endogenous fruit of American social evolution, linked to the country's particular historical experience, and not, as in Europe, a singular measure adopted specifically in relation to the Spanish dispute. The fact is, however, that it notably restricted gestures of adhesion to and solidarity with one side. Moral, intellectual, and political support was freely allowed, of course, as was fundraising for humanitarian purposes, but economic aid directly intended for the contending parties was prohibited, and selling arms to either side was absolutely proscribed. As the war in Spain advanced, these positions evolved. When the support that Franco was receiving from Nazi Germany and Fascist Italy became evident, the possibility of attenuating the rigor of the neutrality laws by authorizing the sale of arms to the Republic began to be seriously considered in the United States.

In any event, throughout 1938, President Roosevelt dismissed the possibility of modifying the neutrality laws in effect for the purpose of carving out an exception for the Spanish case. He did so, probably, thinking about the Catholic vote, which at that time was influenced by the position of the hierarchy and its media allies, who were almost unanimously against altering the U.S. status of neutrality with regard to that conflict, declaring their opposition to lifting the embargo. Very significantly, in November of that year, Antón Irala wrote to Lehendakari Aguirre indicating that even if "the only one who will be able to do something for democratic Spain is Roosevelt," things were complicated because "the date is approaching on which the term set by the Embargo Act expires, and the Catholics (Jesuits) are preparing to prevent it from being lifted."[11] Three months later, Ramón Sota reported that a few days earlier, "the Catholics sent more than a hundred thousand protest telegrams to the Capitol in a single day, because the Senate is considering lifting the embargo. As might be supposed, this has whipped up the campaign by the Catholics, and all their organizations are today spending millions of dollars on propaganda against lifting it."[12]

As Tusell and García Queipo de Llano note, "an American Catholic's initial spontaneous reaction to the events in Spain was likely to be contrary to the insurgents," and if a current of sympathy for Franco did exist, it was probably produced "by the religious persecution that immediately appeared in the press and that made a greater impression in the United States than in the Old World."[13] It should not be forgotten that U.S. society was particularly sensitive to claims associated with freedom of conscience and freedom of worship, because religious freedom was among the founding principles of American democracy. This factor weighed notably on the positions of all concerned because it was well supported by a propaganda campaign that gave blunt accounts of some of the excesses committed in the republican zone, generating a current of solidarity and sympathy toward the insurgents. This current of solidarity, however, never translated into explicit support for the authoritarian forms of government for which the rebels fought. What is more, the two leading figures of the NCWC, Monsignor Ready and Montavon, "always started from the basic assumption that their mission was to defend the Spanish Church and the Catholics, but they made an effort to distinguish this attitude from identification with Franco's cause pure and simple."[14]

In American society at the time, the concepts of democracy and freedom were almost sacred. The problem was that the distance, the general unfamiliarity with Spanish reality, the unique American political culture (so different from its European counterparts in many regards), and the habitual distortion of reports coming from Spain by the insurgents' propa-

---

11. Letter from Irala to Aguirre, New York, October 5, 1938, in San Sebastian, *The Basque Archives*, 203.

12. Letter from Ramón Sota to Aguirre, New York, January 22, 1939, in ibid., 257.

13. Tusell and Garcia Queipo De Llano, *El catolicismo mundial y la guerra de España*, 311.

14. Ibid., 314.

ganda machine caused Franco and his regime to be seen as something very different from what they really stood for.

In sum, the Spanish conflict, so multifaceted and full of nuances, had a complexity that was not easily assimilated to the cultural frameworks and political assumptions of the average American. Propaganda made it even more difficult for the broad American public to acquire an accurate understanding of the war, and in this context, the specific case of the Catholic Basques, which required a particular capacity for discernment to understand, formed another element in an already overly labyrinthine scene.

The United States as a Propaganda Battlefield for the Rebel and Republican Camps

A few months after the conflict began, Largo Caballero's government named Fernando de los Ríos as Spain's ambassador in Washington, D.C. Widely recognized for his intellectual stature and his intense work as a university professor of law, De los Ríos was chosen by the Republic in view of the advantages of his prestige—he was at that time rector of the University of Madrid—and his air of moderation for a diplomatic post that had to be filled with special care. Once the placet had been granted, which was done with particular rapidity, De los Ríos was named ambassador on September 19, 1936.

From the beginning, the new ambassador conceived of his responsibilities in the United States as eminently a propaganda effort aimed at persuading the American authorities and public opinion that the war underway in Spain was not a civil conflict properly speaking, but rather a battle of profound geostrategic significance, in which Hitler's Germany and Mussolini's Italy were resolutely fighting to alter the political equilibrium of Europe in favor of authoritarian ideologies.[15] This was the message he conveyed in his first contacts, both with President Roosevelt, when presenting his credentials, and with the secretary of state. Likewise, this was the content of his first statements to the American press and the talks

---

15. See Virgilio Zapatero, *Fernando de los Ríos: Biografía intelectual* (Valencia: Pre-Textos; Granada: Diputación de Granada, 1999), 416ff, whom we follow in our discussion of this point. On Fernando de los Ríos's activities at the head of the Republic's embassy in Washington, D.C., see also Octavio Ruiz Manjón, *Fernando de los Ríos: Un intelectual en el PSOE* (Madrid: Síntesis, 2007), and Soledad Fox, "Misión imposible: La embajada en Washington de Fernando de los Ríos," in *Al servicio de la República: Diplomáticos y guerra civil,* ed. Ángel Viñas (Madrid: Ministerio de Asuntos Exteriores y de Cooperación; Marcial Pons Historia, 2010), 155–75.

and lectures with which he began his residence in that country. What was taking place in Spain was not a confrontation between Catholics and atheists, but rather "the first act of a drama of universal dimensions," in which the principles of the Enlightenment were in open conflict with the idea of absolute power.

He soon realized the need to launch an information and propaganda service capable of influencing American public opinion, inducing it to adopt this conception of the Spanish war. For that purpose, the Spanish Information Bureau was created in New York, in charge of publishing the magazine *News of Spain* and all kinds of pamphlets in favor of the republican side. As De los Rios himself indicated in a letter dated August 1937, the New York bureau carried out a colossal labor in the information and propaganda sphere:

> It composes a report for the press each day, publishes information sheets and pamphlets (sometimes propaganda ones), and publishes and distributes pamphlets like the one by Fischer, *The War of Spain* (even if it appears as a publication of *The Nation* as a way to keep it from appearing as a propaganda piece). It's now preparing the English translation of the white paper on the Italian intervention in order to send it to all the congressmen and senators, a trip to Spain by a congressional delegation, a new edition of the speeches I've given in this country, a pamphlet on the German, Italian, and Portuguese intervention, and another pamphlet on religious persecution by fascism in Italy, Germany, and Spain. Occasionally, it organizes a radio lecture.[16]

In addition, the embassy also promoted and financed the publication of the daily newspaper *La Voz*, published in Spanish. Its influence on the Spanish-speaking population is evidenced in the reports sent from New York to Salamanca by Franco's delegate, who accused it, with undisguised displeasure, of defending the Valencia regime "at all costs," including "more or less falsified news about Spain," and providing "extensive information about the activities of the Reds in this country." The most worrisome aspect of its informational line, nonetheless, from the perspective of Franco's supporters, was the fact that it "frequently" sought "to sound the alarm that the Spanish war was becoming a world war provoked by the world's fascist elements."[17]

---

16. Zapatero, *Fernando de los Ríos*, 438–39.

17. AMAE R-598, press summary corresponding to the month of November, in letter from Cárdenas to the general secretary of foreign relations, December 14, 1937, 9.

De los Ríos was quite effective in the academic sphere. He gave lectures at various universities and promoted the publication of manifestos in favor of the republican cause signed by eminent figures of the academic world—most notably Einstein—and American public life. His activity on this terrain was intense and untiring. Nevertheless, he was not able to prevent the inexorable application of the Neutrality Act, which opted for non-intervention and authorized the president, in the event of war, to declare an arms embargo against any belligerent country. Despite Roosevelt's personal appreciation for De los Ríos and the cause he represented, in late 1936 he commissioned several members of Congress to draw up an amendment to the Neutrality Act that would prohibit arms exports to war-torn Spain.

De los Ríos insisted on the idea that Franco's potential triumph in Spain might arouse the sympathy of the Latin American countries for dictatorial political formulas, to the detriment of U.S. interests. However, nothing altered the firmness with which Roosevelt demanded the Neutrality Act's application. The attitude taken by Great Britain—which habitually conditioned U.S. positions with regard to Europe—and the scant sympathy for the republican cause professed by the majority of American Catholics, who constituted one of President Roosevelt's chief electoral bases, did not make it easy for him to translate his support for the loyalist side into concrete acts.

On the opposite side from De los Ríos, and in open propaganda opposition to him, was Juan Francisco de Cárdenas y Rodríguez de Rivas, who acted as Franco's unofficial delegate to the United States beginning in the first months of 1937. When the civil war broke out, Cárdenas was Spain's ambassador in Paris, a diplomatic post he had held since being transferred from Washington, D.C., in 1934 to replace Salvador de Madariaga. Only two days after the uprising, Prime Minister José Giral, a republican, assigned him the delicate task of seeking from the French executive the delivery of arms to reinforce the republican army's military equipment. Although Cárdenas sympathized with the rebels, he punctually carried out the prime minister's order, persuaded that the French response would be negative. As soon as he found out that French Prime Minister Léon Blum's government was disposed to accede to the Spanish request, however, he submitted his resignation and disappeared from the scene.

A few months later, Cárdenas reappeared in the United States—where he had served as a diplomat in the past,[18] enabling him to make contacts and build relationships that would be very useful to him in his new mission—with the aim of acting as the rebels' diplomatic representative. No sooner had Cárdenas disembarked in the United States than he promoted the formation of a Defense Board (Junta de Defensa), into which he integrated, by his own account, "a group of patriotic Spaniards who had already met previously to work for the Cause."[19] The board acted as the representative of the Burgos cabinet until November 1936, when Cárdenas was given the task of setting up an unofficial diplomatic representation for the rebels, in order to "direct and centralize all activities pursued here in favor of the Cause."

However, the legalization of his presence in the country had to overcome certain obstacles. In May 1937, he was accused by Senator Nye from North Dakota of engaging in espionage on behalf of "General Franco and his fascist state." The accusation was publicized by the *Daily Worker* and other communications media. Cárdenas suspected from the beginning that "De los Ríos with his North American Committee to Aid Spanish Democracy" was behind the maneuver.[20] The charge concerned him, because his residence in the United States was based on a tourist visa that had expired on May 17 of that year.

After seeking advice on the situation from various lawyers, Cárdenas rejected the idea of cooperating with an official investigation by the upper house, because "the atmosphere in the Senate is, in general, unfavorable to us," and as a consequence, "in the best of cases, it would be very harsh toward us and very indulgent toward our opponents, since they are considered the 'legal government' here and since they have the sympathy of the press and a large part of public opinion."[21]

Cárdenas also had other concerns: "If it is going to be an investigation in bad faith," he noted, "it would always be easy to muddle things so that

18. Cárdenas was Spain's ambassador in Washington from 1932 to 1934, but he had already held various posts in the Spanish legation prior to those dates.

19. AMAE R-598, letter from Cárdenas to Don Manuel Arias Paz, press and propaganda delegate in Salamanca, New York, October 15, 1937 (text no. 18), 12.

20. AMAE R-598, letter from Cárdenas to the general secretary of foreign relations, New York, May 12, 1937.

21. AMAE R-598, letter from Cárdenas to the general secretary of foreign relations, New York, May 27, 1937.

they did not appear clearly and to give rise to dangerous and slanderous suspicions, especially taking into account that I am not at all inclined to turn over my files, since if the names of patriots sympathetic to the Cause were revealed, it would expose them to reprisals."[22]

In the end, Franco's delegate was able to normalize his situation, albeit by accommodating to the conditions imposed by the State Department, which categorically prohibited him from using in his title the word "government," or any other that referred to representation of a possibly diplomatic or consular nature. He was authorized to use the title of "agent" on condition that it was not accompanied by the term "government." The State Department suggested the title of "Agent of the Nationalist Forces."[23] He ultimately submitted his paperwork using the title of "Agent of Generalísimo Franco and His Authorities." On December 27, 1937, the State Department acknowledged receipt of the notification, warning Cárdenas that the recognition that had been granted to him did not confer official status in the United States, due to the fact that the federal government had not recognized the regime as the petitioner. The situation was not ideal, but the offer was accepted.

Like De los Ríos, Cárdenas designed a plan that put special emphasis on the tasks of information and propaganda, deemed all the more necessary when it was a matter of trying to prevent confusion and to influence the U.S. public, "little given on its own to reflection and to drawing distinctions."[24] In June 1937, he intercepted a letter sent from the republican embassy requesting collaboration and support from a member of the Institute for Social Research at Columbia University. The aim was to counteract the "intensive and intelligent propaganda campaign" that Franco's sympathizers had carried out in the Baltimore-Washington, D.C., area through a pro-Spain public event. The news confirmed Franco's agent in the conviction that his gamble was the correct one: propaganda was one of the chief tools for action in the United States.

Cárdenas based his communications plan on two foundations. First, he carried out a highly noteworthy effort to exhaustively study the American media market. Only complete knowledge of the media, their ideologi-

---

22. Ibid.

23. AMAE R-598, letter from Cárdenas to José Antonio Sangróniz, head of Franco's diplomatic cabinet, New York, November 19, 1937.

24. AMAE R-598, press summary for the month of July, in letter from Cárdenas to the general secretary of foreign relations, New York, August 6, 1937, p. 6.

cal inclinations, and their editorial lines would make it possible to design effective propaganda that would fill in the gaps of the local press, reinforce reports favorable to the insurgents, and attempt to neutralize those contrary to them. However, it was not enough to be familiar with the U.S. media universe. It was also a matter of influencing it, with the aim of improving the rebels' position in U.S. public opinion. To that end, Cárdenas launched a communications office that, directly dependent on the Salamanca Press Delegation, concerned itself with designing and coordinating Falangist information and propaganda in the United States. We will review both aspects.

At the request of the Salamanca Propaganda and Press Office, Cárdenas drew up a memorandum in which he sketched a quite detailed portrait of the U.S. print press, specifying the attitude of each media outlet regarding the Spanish military conflict.[25] His initial findings could not have been less promising for interests of rebel propaganda: "In general," the document laconically affirmed, "it can be said that the attitude of the American press has at no time been favorable to the National Movement." In this dark panorama, Cárdenas's enthusiasm picked out small points of light, but he could not fail to acknowledge the lack of newspapers "of relative importance, except for those that call themselves Catholic, [of which] it can be said that they openly defend our cause."[26]

Their fundamental reason for taking this position was not rooted, in Cárdenas's judgment, in the democratic inclinations that the American media perceived in the government of the Republic, but rather in the influence of the Jewish community, which was clearly aligned against the rebels' fascist allies: "the newspapers depend on their advertisers, whom the news agencies have to keep happy, and the advertisers, the majority of whom are Jews, are opposed to General Franco's regime, especially since his name has become so closely associated with those of Hitler and Mussolini."[27]

Many editors, Cárdenas affirmed, were personally sympathetic to Franco, but did not dare to declare that sympathy openly out of fear that Jewish advertisers would withdraw their ads, that the labor unions would go on strike, and that there might be reprisals from the political parties and the Roosevelt administration, all of whom were "frankly favorable, for

25. AMAE R-598, memorandum, New York, August 12, 1937.

26. Ibid., 2.

27. Ibid., 3.

the moment, to those whom they always call 'loyalists' here." This scene had only one exception, the Catholic press, where papers were to be found that defended "the true Cause of Spain with the greatest determination and bravery, as if it were their own affair." As we will see in the following pages, the periodic reports that Cárdenas sent to Salamanca were dedicated to reproducing this same perception, with little variation and very limited evolution.

Throughout 1937, Franco's special agent dedicated most of his time to the attentive examination of the American press, and every month he sent a report to the General Secretariat of Foreign Relations giving a detailed account of the impact of news from the civil war on public opinion and the communications media in the United States. His initial impressions confirmed the fact that the country's most important daily newspapers had taken "a position of more or less open sympathy for the Reds, although trying to avoid any praise or encouragement for the doctrines that have been put into practice in the zone ruled by Madrid, Barcelona, and Valencia."[28] This initial perception was strengthened with the passage of time, in such a way that, when the first anniversary of the coup d'état against the Republic came around, Franco's agent lamented the fact that "almost all" the newspapers "have once again shown how mistaken they are and how deeply unfamiliar with the patriotic and humane meaning of the glorious Nationalist rebellion."[29] The series of quotations collected in this document were certainly discouraging for an enthusiast—as Cárdenas undoubtedly was— of Franco's cause. Among the examples he provides, a *New York Times* editorial published on July 21, 1937, stands out. Titled "A Year of Triumph," it summarizes the achievements of the rebels as follows:

> Dozens of Guernicas bombed until not a stone remains upon a stone; hundreds of thousands of Spaniards brutally killed, including an uncounted number of women and children; national monuments destroyed that can never be replaced . . . these are the victories illuminating General FRANCO's "year of triumph." . . . If this tortured and riven land, this holocaust of unknown dead, this terror of the living, this exile of reason and pity, represents triumph, it

---

28. AMAE R-598, press summary for the month of April, in letter from Cárdenas to the general secretary of foreign relations, New York, May 2, 1937, 1.

29. AMAE R-598, press summary for the month of July, in letter from Cárdenas to the general secretary of foreign relations, New York, August 6, 1937, 3.

must be the kind of triumph celebrated in hell. For Spain it has been a year of agony, ruin and defeat.[30]

Nevertheless, the scene was different among Catholic-inspired publications, in whose pages—Cárdenas observed with undisguised satisfaction—"the Spanish case has come to be almost uniformly presented in a manner favorable to the Nationalists, although some important magazines have not succeeded in shaking off the influence exercised on them by the confusion of the revolution's first days and by their complete unfamiliarity with conditions in Spain before and after last July." In this regard, Franco's agent celebrated the fact that some Catholic magazines that had at first hesitated had gradually, with the passage of time and the evolution of events, become "defenders and paladins" of the rebel cause. Cárdenas observed that "in every issue, they insist on warning their readers of the dangers approaching this country if the communist advance is not quickly and effectively checked, expressing the fear that what is happening now in Spain might one day happen in the United States." In his reports, the evaluation that "almost all of the Catholic press sympathizes with and defends the Nationalist Cause" is almost constant. Not all of that press acted in the same way or had the same effect on public opinion, however. Among the handful of Catholic-inspired publications on the American market, Cárdenas's reports showed particular enthusiasm for two: *The Brooklyn Tablet*, the unofficial organ of the diocese of Brooklyn, which was "on the front line" of the defense of the "Nationalist Cause," and the magazine *America*.

With irrepressible satisfaction, Cárdenas said of *The Brooklyn Tablet*'s director, Patrick Scanlan, that "he does not let pass the least opportunity to refute the slanders and falsehoods against the true Spain and does not shrink from becoming involved in polemics with the publications that defend the Reds . . . he is always ready to defend the truth, employing a style that is at times harsh and severe, but always clear, and in any event, his affirmations usually prevail, by means of the polemics aroused by his enthusiastic defense of the Nationalist Cause."

Due to this belligerence by its chief, *The Brooklyn Tablet* came to have a notable impact and influence on the American view of the Spanish conflict, because some editors, Cárdenas said, "little familiar with the facts

---

30. "Year of Triumph," editorial, *New York Times*, July 21, 1937, 20; AMAE R-598, press summary for the month of July, in letter from Cárdenas to the general secretary of foreign relations, New York, August 6, 1937, 4.

of the Spanish conflict, find it difficult to escape from the well-supported attacks of the *Tablet*'s director and do not want to expose themselves to the risk of an attack or a polemic with an expert enemy who knows the material and expounds the facts very freely and frankly."[31] As a result of all this, Franco's agent did not hesitate to attribute to this publication the title of "the great champion of nationalism," an honor it shared in his view with the magazine *America,* published by the New York Jesuits, and its director Father Talbot, for whom Cárdenas had only praise and good wishes.[32]

Cárdenas did not hide his satisfaction each time that the belligerent Catholic media won a public-opinion battle in defense of the thesis that "the so-called loyalist cause in Spain has been predominantly communist and anarchist."[33] That was, in his opinion, the vision of the war in Spain that needed to be publicized in the United States. Nevertheless, he noted unhappily that the Catholic publications had a very modest influence on public opinion, since their small press runs did not permit mass diffusion: "their circulation," he observed, "cannot be compared, unfortunately, with that of the opposing publications, and this disadvantage is accentuated by the fact that they only come into the hands of the Catholics, and not those of the Reds, who might thereby be informed of the truth and perhaps rectify their views, while the Red magazines are read by many persons on the right, whom that propaganda, so intensely practiced and powerfully organized, occasionally does not fail to impress."[34] In the Protestant and Jewish press, on the other hand, the weight of sympathy was predominantly in favor of the Republic. The media universe was prone to interpret the Spanish conflict as a confrontation between democracy and fascism.

---

31. AMAE R-598, press summary for the month of July, in letter from Cárdenas to the general secretary of foreign relations, New York, August 6, 1937, 14–15.

32. The unconditional allegiance professed by Father Talbot and his magazine *America* to the rebel cause is indicated by the following comment included by Manu Sota in his report on American Catholicism. *America* was, in his judgment, "a Falangist propaganda libel, prodigious in slanderous falsehoods, and in which there was even published a poem, from the pen of another Jesuit, Father Feeney, with the following sacrilegious refrain: 'Oh Jesus, oh God, oh Franco.' This will explain better than anything else the spiritual ilk of the director of *America,* perhaps the magazine with the most distinguished heritage in the diminutive U.S. Catholic world, in which Father Talbot is a star of the first magnitude." Analysis of the position of the Catholics of the United States in relation to the European war, New York, May 7, 1940 (Archivo Iñaki Anasagasti, Fondo Delegación EEUU, 4.)

33. AMAE R-598, press summary for the month of May, in letter from Cárdenas to the general secretary of foreign relations, New York, June 4, 1937, 2.

34. AMAE R-598, press summary for the month of July, in letter from Cárdenas to the general secretary of foreign relations, New York, August 6, 1937, 17.

Toward the end of 1937, Cárdenas's reports referred with special concern to the support for the republican cause in the Washington, D.C., press. The city's press remained firm "in its attitude of underlining the part played by Germany and Italy in the Spanish Civil War, thereby disposing the public against the National Movement," in view of the enormous weight in American public opinion of the idea of fighting against the dictatorial European powers, "for the purpose of saving democracy." In this regard, Cárdenas observed a worrisome evolution in the informational line marked out by the capital's press, one frankly hostile to the rebels' propaganda interests: "almost all those who openly defended the Valencia government before do so now from the perspective of the German-Italian intervention only, while the newspapers that favored us as opponents of communism, criticizing the Red government as a representative of that ideology, are coming to present a disposition identical to that of their other colleagues, since as an expression of American patriotism, they have accentuated their attack on those powers that are, according to them, just as much enemies of American democratic institutions as communism is, or that, like Japan, represent a threat to this country's interests."[35] Despite everything, Cárdenas considered that the U.S. public was "coming to understand, despite the press," that there was something "fundamentally unacceptable on the side of the Valencia regime," and that, as a consequence, it should not be supported "under the title of defending democracy."[36]

However, the press, especially the Washington, D.C., press, refused to budge. In December 1937, Cárdenas again confirmed that "the tone of the Washington press is even more unfavorable than that of New York," noting that the editorials, with the occasional exception, "are all unfavorable, either directly or indirectly, and as far as the articles, they are almost exclusively opposed."[37]

The favorable evolution of the war led Cárdenas to emphasize the optimistic side. He thought that "first of all, and above all, the one hundred and twenty-six million Americans are nothing more than merchants, and the

---

35. AMAE R-598, Washington press summary corresponding to the month of November, in letter from Cárdenas to the general secretary of foreign relations, dated New York, December 21, 1937, 2–3.

36. AMAE R-598, press summary corresponding to the month of November, in letter from Cárdenas to the general secretary of foreign relations, December 14, 1937, 2.

37. AMAE R-598, Washington press summary corresponding to the month of December, dated New York, January 19, 1938, 8.

only thing that matters to them is being on good terms with whomever is in charge or will be in charge in the different countries."[38]

For purposes of this study, it must be noted that some of Cárdenas's reports paid special attention to the media echo produced by the bombing of Gernika. Specifically, he lamented that the bombing had been presented as "the work of the Germans, and trying to incite a sentiment of universal protest against the event, insisting that the Reds have not engaged in analogous actions," and that after the story was corrected, when it became known "that there was no bombing, but rather a fire set by the communists, as in Irun and Eibar," the media had suppressed or trimmed the information. He also noted the tendency of a certain sector of the press to sympathize with the "priests and religious figures who have taken the side of the Reds and the Basque separatists," whose names were repeated as those of heroes, martyrs, and eminent figures of the Church, who were supporting the people in the "struggle for their freedom and for democracy." In the case of Gernika, he had to settle for the understanding of the Catholic press, since "most of the dailies have not wanted to accept the Nationalist account that it was the work of Red dynamiters." Only the Catholic media had "accused the Reds."[39]

He also paid special attention to those who dedicated themselves to presenting "the sophism of Basque nationalist Catholics allied with the Red government, in order to draw the conclusion that the Catholics are and should be against General Franco's Nationalist Movement."[40] In his report for June 1937, he complained that the press had focused on the "destruction of some Basque cities by Aguirre's troops, falsely attributed to the Nationalist army, with the aim of creating separatist sympathies,"[41] and in this regard, he observed, "With reference to the burning and destruction of Basque cities, there has been an attempt to shape a legend of heroism and patriotic grandeur around the figure of Aguirre, always making note

38. AMAE R-598, report on the Washington press, August 13, 1937, 10.

39. AMAE R-598, press summary for the month of June, in letter from Cárdenas to the general secretary of foreign relations, July 5, 1937, 2.

40. AMAE R-598, press summary for the month of May, in letter from Cárdenas to the general secretary of foreign relations, June 4, 1937, 3.

41. AMAE R-598, press summary for the month of June, in letter from Cárdenas to the general secretary of foreign relations, July 5, 1937, 1.

of his status as a 'fervent Catholic' in order to continue with the mistaken idea that the Catholics are with the Reds of Valencia."[42]

Cárdenas also dedicated significant effort to reporting on the polemic roused in the American press and public opinion regarding the Basque children sent by the Republic to other countries, with the aim of putting them beyond reach of the dangers of the war. In a letter dated mid-June 1937, Cárdenas applauded the fact that the plans of the American Board of Guardians for Basque Children were to a large extent frustrated by the contrary efforts of a Massachusetts congressman named John W. McCormack, who warned of the possibility that young children brought up as Catholics might be exposed to the pernicious influence of "communist propaganda," and by the publicly expressed opposition of President Roosevelt's wife, who considered it "inappropriate to bring over Basque children" for the purpose of integrating them into "a country that is not their own and is completely different from the environment in which they have grown up."[43] He also lashed out repeatedly against the New York Times correspondent in Madrid, well-known journalist Herbert L. Matthews, for whom he did not express a great deal of sympathy, given his "profound adhesion to the Reds."

Cárdenas closely followed Ambassador de los Ríos, whose activities he reported punctually to Salamanca, at the same time recounting their echo in the American press. In May 1937 he reported that De los Ríos "is continuing his campaign of defamation against the Catholic Church, attending several Red demonstrations at which he does not cease to attack all that is traditionally Spanish."[44] Likewise, Cárdenas identified him as the chief inspiration of the informational line followed by the Washington Post regarding the civil war. He repeated on more than one occasion that this was a daily newspaper "intimately united to the Red embassy"[45] or "very much influenced by the Red ambassador De los Ríos."[46]

---

42. Ibid.

43. AMAE R-598, letter from Cárdenas to the general secretary of foreign relations, New York, June 17, 1937.

44. AMAE R-598, press summary for the month of May, in letter from Cárdenas to the general secretary of foreign relations, June 4, 1937, 8.

45. For example, in AMAE R-598, press summary corresponding to the month of November, in letter from Cárdenas to the general secretary of foreign relations, December 21, 1937, 2.

46. AMAE R-598, Washington press summary corresponding to the month of December, dated New York, January 19, 1938, 1.

As we have noted above, Cárdenas also organized a communications office with the aim of transmitting the messages and articles put out by the press and propaganda authorities based in Salamanca to American public opinion, the heart of his mission in the United States. As he put it in a letter sent in October 1937, the office was at that date "in a period of organization," but that had not prevented Falangist propaganda in America from flowing with notable intensity, because "propaganda work has been done since this representation was established."[47] Due to Washington's importance in shaping public opinion, Cárdenas sent Miguel Echegaray there "to direct, monitor, and distribute our propaganda, especially in that sector." He soon brought him back, however, to work with José Pedroso. From Philadelphia, Pedroso was a former president of the Defense Board set up in the United States in support of the July 18, 1936, military uprising in Spain, and with his collaboration, Echegaray was to direct the office's initial nucleus, "as an independent body, but always dependent" on Cárdenas. This original cell was gradually expanded, thanks to the collaboration of other friendly media and the donations received. In October 1937, it was much more than merely a project sketched on paper. As Cárdenas reported to Salamanca, "in fact, the office is already functioning, lacking only a publicity agent and the ability to work in the light of day."[48]

A few weeks later, the office completed the bureaucratic procedures required to work "in the light of day." It did so by incorporating under American law, as the Peninsular News Service, Inc. One of the office's first objectives consisted in publishing a magazine that would bring to the American reader "the ideas of National Spain, its struggle, its principles, and its work of reconstruction," something that Cárdenas considered indispensable, "since the press here is Red in its entirety."[49] This idea gave rise to the magazine *Spain*.

From an operational point of view, Franco's agent believed that an organ of this kind would make it possible to "provide the appropriate information about National Spain in journalistic form, an outlet for the photographic material, and needed replies at the opportune time." Cárdenas proposed a biweekly publication, not a weekly as proposed in Salamanca, so that

47. AMAE R-598, letter from Cárdenas to Don Manuel Arias Paz, press and propaganda delegate in Salamanca, New York, October 15, 1937 (text no. 18), 1.

48. Ibid., 14.

49. AMAE R-598, letter from Cárdenas to Manuel Arias Paz, press and propaganda delegate in Salamanca, New York, October 15, 1937, 1.

the high cost of paper and salaries would not result in a single publication consuming more than half of the office's monthly budget. A biweekly publication, on the other hand, would make it possible to select the information more carefully and not include "those points that, although of interest, would not be advantageous to discuss for various reasons."

What kind of information was Cárdenas referring to when he put forward the need to hide certain points from American public opinion? Franco's special agent himself explains in the following lines:

> for the time being, let's not publish those articles that might contribute to depicting our Movement as an exclusively fascist one, since all the Red propaganda campaigns in this country work by trying to present the Civil War in Spain as a struggle between fascism and democracy, and we would thereby give them an opening to intensify their propaganda along these lines. Our propaganda campaign should be 'order and civilization against communism and anarchy,' 'Christianity against the godless and irreligious,' 'communism kills democracy.' Later on, it will be possible to find space in our magazine for articles of that type that it would not be politic to publish today.[50]

Clearly, Cárdenas did not consider it advantageous to associate the rebels' image with that of the European fascist powers, at least not before an American audience that was frankly repulsed by fascist movements. Doing so would mean earning the hostility of U.S. public opinion. For this reason, Cárdenas put forward the advisability of avoiding that image. Spaniards residing in the United States had to be told the truth; they had to gradually be made familiar "with the absolute ideas of the Movement." There was no reason, however, that this function should be assigned to the magazine *Spain,* which was conceived for an American audience. It could be the task of another publication, titled *Cara al sol* [Face to the Sun], a weekly sheet that was being published "by some enthusiastic young Spaniards with our help." The two publications complemented one another, offering each reader what it was advantageous to give him.

The first issue of *Spain* came out in October 1937 and took advantage of the coincidence with Columbus Day to focus special attention on the figure of Christopher Columbus.

---

50. Ibid., 3.

The Work of the Euzkadi Government's Delegation

The social and political reality sketched in the preceding sections formed the stage on which the delegation sent to New York by Lehendakari Aguirre in mid-1938 would have to act, and in the context described, it was not particularly complicated to define the objectives that its mission would have to pursue. It seemed obvious that the delegation should focus its attention on the Catholic community. It was precisely this American social group on which the delegation could act most effectively with a view toward increasing support for the republican side.

Two arguments backed this strategy. The members of the delegation professed the Roman Catholic faith and were acting in the name of a cabinet whose president, a Catholic activist from his earliest youth, had made visible gestures of public adhesion to the values and principles of Christianity. On the other hand, Catholics were the American social group most clearly under the influence of Franco's propaganda and in which the lowest levels of support for the legitimate government were found.

An explanation of the reasons that had led a majority-Catholic political movement such as Basque nationalism to decide to close ranks against Franco's army might be very useful in encouraging those U.S. groups with ties to the Roman Church to critically review their positions with regard to the civil war, overcoming the received ideas and oversimplifications that ignorance, disinformation, and the manipulation of reality had caused them to embrace up to that point.

The Preliminary Steps

President Aguirre realized very early on the potential importance of opening a delegation in the United States that could serve as a platform for extending to American society the Basque government's propaganda effort. The Basque government was engaged in a similar campaign in Europe in order to defend the Basque national cause and successfully explain the choice of the Catholic Basque nationalists in favor of the republican side. Nevertheless, the need to respond to other, more urgent needs meant that the idea could not take material form until mid-1938. During the preceding months, the Lehendakari meditated extensively on the project, and after soliciting other perspectives, he promoted a series of initiatives intended to make it possible to put the idea into practice with a guarantee of success.

The first step consisted in selecting the individuals who were going to make up the delegation. The task was a delicate one because the success of the mission depended in large part on the selection of the delegation members. Aguirre had in mind a small but highly qualified group that could be expanded with new personnel later. To begin with, the office would be inaugurated by three men: Antón Irala, Manu Sota, and the latter's nephew, Ramón de la Sota MacMahon. The first two were lawyers, and the third had a degree in political and economic sciences, from Cambridge no less, with a specialization in international relations. All three had a good command of English and were, despite their youth, well-read, mature, and well-traveled.

Once the members of the delegation had been chosen, Aguirre turned his attention to giving the project shape. First, he resolved to enlist the support of the U.S. ambassador to the Republic, Claude G. Bowers, who had been operating out of the Hotel Miramar in Donibane Lohizune since the beginning of the civil war. For this purpose, the Lehendakari made use of the good offices of Manuel Inchausti, the generous Basque Maecenas, whose large network of relationships included a wide and select representation of the diplomatic world. In addition, Inchausti had always enjoyed notable influence in American institutional circles; it was not in vain that he boasted U.S. nationality and was in direct contact with former President William Howard Taft, of whose brother Henry he was a personal friend.

Bowers, of course, agreed to Inchausti's request, and on July 26, 1938, he wrote to the U.S. consul-general in Paris, Robert D. Murphy, personally endorsing the solvency and trustworthiness of the three men who were to make up the Basque delegation and requesting his assistance for a rapid handling of the matter. With regard to Manu Sota, he highlighted his status, and with regard to all three, he affirmed their good reputations for which reason he asked his colleague to facilitate the process of getting the visas issued quickly.[51] Bowers's recommendation produced excellent results. The U.S. consulate-general in Paris was extremely diligent in handling the documentation needed by the future members of the delegation with all possible speed. By August 2, Irala already had his papers in order and informed Inchausti with satisfaction that the American legation in Paris had given him "facilities of all kinds" in arranging "everything having to do with my passport."[52] Manu Sota's documents would take slightly longer,

---

51. Letter from Bowers to Murphy, Donibane Lohizune, July 26, 1938 (Archivo Iñaki Anasagasti, Fondo Delegación EEUU).

52. Letter from Irala to Inchausti, Paris, August 2, 1938 (Archivo Iñaki Anasagasti, Fondo Delegación EEUU).

but not for reasons attributable to the American consulate, but rather due to the "lack of something needed from the Spanish representation."[53] For his part, Ramón Sota, who was in London, had been able to resolve everything in the British capital, because "he will surely embark in England."

Paying heed to Inchausti's suggestion, Bowers also promised to write to the American secretary of state, Cordell Hull, asking him to receive and give a hearing to the Basque delegation. On this point, nevertheless, he warned Inchausti about the advisability of notifying the Republic's ambassador in Washington, De los Ríos, arguing that "in Spanish affairs" the secretary of state "obviously deals in the first instance with the Spanish ambassador, and the latter could consider it a discourtesy to discuss his affair without his knowledge." Bowers assured Inchausti that the Basque delegation "was not going to encounter difficulties" in making contacts at the State Department, but he warned, with the insight appropriate to an experienced diplomat, that "it is important that we take care not to cause the impression in Washington that there is any conflict between the Basques and the Spanish government."[54]

Following Bowers's suggestions, the Lehendakari wrote a very friendly and courteous letter to De los Ríos for Irala and Manu Sota to give to the ambassador in person as soon as they had occasion to visit him in Washington, D.C. The missive's text clearly described the propaganda project being pursued by Aguirre—who desired to extend to the United States the experiment implemented in Europe—and his intention to carry it out in coordination, of course, with the authorities of the Republic, but through formally independent channels, so that his message could have a more intense impact on the Catholic sectors, some of which were clearly predisposed against the Republic because of the excesses committed against the Church from within its camp. The efficacy of the mission, which was of interest to all, demanded that the Basque government's activity be formally separate from that promoted by the republican authorities, without prejudice to the mutual loyalty that had to preside over the relationship between

---

53. As Irala wrote to Sota himself, the problem was due to the fact that his passport expired in two months, and "in the United States there is a law according to which a foreigner who is going to enter is supposed to leave two months prior to the expiration of his passport . . . For that reason, they don't issue a visa at the consulate, and since it's been noted at the consulate, there's nothing else that can be done other than requesting an extension from the Republic's agencies."

54. Letter from Bowers to Inchausti, Donibane Lohizune, July 26, 1938 (Archivo Iñaki Anasagasti, Fondo Delegación EEUU).

the Basque and Spanish executives. Here are the letter's most significant passages:

> You are aware, Don Fernando, with how much interest I have always wanted to make an entry into America through effective propaganda among that people, of such great interest. You will recall our conversation in Barcelona, precisely in the presence of President Negrín. You already know the form in which we have acted in France, in Belgium, and in England, as well as in other countries, with evident profit for our Basque People and for the Republic. For this reason, this propaganda has to be carried out independently by the Basque organization, in order to gain entry into those circles which we have penetrated in Europe and have to penetrate in America. This conceptual independence, due to our special idiosyncrasy, has to be intimately linked to you, as ambassador of the Republic, but without the intervention of the bodies that depend on it, directly or indirectly. You know well that in this, we are seeking effectiveness, which as in Paris and London, I hope to obtain in the United States as well.
>
> Our chief concern is the Catholic milieu, by way of the immediate publication of works that here, in Europe, have made a deep impression and attracted abundant critical attention, in the most favorable terms, of course.[55]

With the objective of avoiding prejudices and suspicions that might ultimately cause serious harm to their shared interests, Aguirre informed the Republic's ambassador in Washington, D.C., of the orders he had given to the members of the Basque delegation for the purpose of guaranteeing mutual loyalty and coordination of activities. Aguirre asked the ambassador to intervene with the organizations aligned with the Republic in order that they not show themselves hostile to the Basque executive's delegates.

> Messieurs Irala and De la Sota have specific instructions to keep you informed of everything that they do and of the results and impressions they obtain. I have no need to ask the same of you. I know that in return, you will receive them with the warmth that you have always shown toward our affairs . . .
>
> It is very important that the organizations supportive of the Republic that are active there be discreetly advised of the purpose of our envoys, so that they do not see them as a foreign mission, but rather one converging on the same ends, even if employing different means, with a view precisely toward the effectiveness of our propaganda.[56]

---

55. Letter from Aguirre to Fernando de los Ríos, Paris, August 12, 1938 (Archivo Iñaki Anasagasti, Fondo Delegación EEUU).

56. Ibid.

In the days prior to the group's embarkation, Aguirre proceeded to make the official appointments. Antón Irala was named "direct delegate of this Presidential Office for propaganda in North America, with extremely wide powers to direct and manage its interests, including financial ones." He was invested as the head of the delegation, such that the other members were subject to "the subordination conferred by the direct representation of this Presidential Office." For his part, Manu Sota was named "responsible for the unlimited management and direction of the artistic and athletic groups and events that the Basque government employs abroad for propaganda purposes."[57] From this time forward, everything was ready to begin the voyage.

At the beginning of August 1938, Irala thought that the delegation's embarkation for New York would take place "one of these days," delayed only by pending paperwork related to the delegation members' documents. Their plan, he reported to Inchausti, was the following: "We'll surely embark on the 10th or the 13th. The *Normandie* leaves on the 10th, and the *Ile de France* on the 13th."[58]

In the end, Irala and Manu Sota left the French coast behind on August 13. By late August, they were already in New York, where they joined forces in order to found the delegation with Ramón Sota, who had crossed the Atlantic on a ship sailing from London. From the delegation, they devoted themselves to carrying out the propaganda mission entrusted to them by the Lehendakari.

With the passage of time, the delegation's initial composition would undergo notable changes. Already in his letter to Fernando de los Ríos, the Lehendakari announced that the inaugural group, made up of three "young and hard-working men," would be only the vanguard of "another commission of greater age and extensive preparation, which will depart as soon as these men have appropriately prepared the terrain." Aguirre was carefully studying the possibility of sending "a priest," among others, and he specified, "The advisability of sending one or not will be determined on the basis of these preliminary studies."[59]

---

57. Accreditation issued in Paris on August 12, 1938 (Archivo Iñaki Anasagasti, Fondo Delegación EEUU).

58. Letter from Irala to Inchausti, Paris, August 2, 1938 (Archivo Iñaki Anasagasti, Fondo Delegación EEUU).

59. Letter from Aguirre to Fernando de los Ríos, Paris, August 12, 1938 (Archivo Iñaki Anasagasti, Fondo Delegación EEUU).

The changes would not be long in coming. In late September 1938, the Lehendakari named the Navarrese journalist Juan Aramburu press officer, "to depend directly on this president's delegate, Don Antonio de Irala, with whom he will handle all matters related to his mission."[60] Shortly thereafter, Aramburu disembarked in New York to join an office in which, for several weeks, he performed an extremely discreet task.

Around the same time, Irala formulated for the Lehendakari a series of reflections by the members of the delegation in relation to its structure and composition. Sooner or later, it would be necessary to arrange an increase in personnel: "if the plan is carried out in full," Irala warned, "the delegation will need to be divided, and someone more would be needed."[61] At the same time, it would be inadvisable to act precipitately or start endowing the delegation with an overly inflated staff without due consideration. On the other hand, the office's staff had to be scrupulously selected. Not just anyone had the right qualities to successfully carry out the work that had to be done there. Knowledge of English was indispensable, but in addition, a certain diplomatic vision and skill dealing with people were also required.

Manu and Ramón Sota thought that Vilallonga and Alejandro Sota, who had apparently been suggested from Paris as possible candidates to increase the delegation's staff, would not be "the best fitted" for that function; "on the other hand, José Urresti would be, due to his personality and aptitudes, which are a perfect match with American psychology." Irala added to this observation a series of considerations of his own:

> As far as we are concerned, I'll also give you my opinion: I believe that Manu and Ramón are indispensable here. They work perfectly and intensely. Manu due to his way of presenting himself, his manner, and the great affection he has for the task you have assigned to him: he has already built relationships that could not be abandoned now. And Ramón due to his perfect command of English and the American friends he has. He also takes care of the correspondence and reports in English. The only one who can be replaced is myself, with a view toward what you decide in the future . . . The best news that you could give Manu, even in the event of war, is that he should be on the next boat . . . he has been homesick for France since the first day we arrived.[62]

---

60. Credential issued in Paris on September 24, 1938 (Archivo Iñaki Anasagasti, Fondo Delegación EEUU).

61. Letter from Irala to Aguirre, New York, September 28, 1938, in San Sebastian, *The Basque Archives*, 199.

62. Ibid.

In October 1938, the Lehendakari began to give shape to the general proposal previously communicated to Ambassador Fernando de los Ríos in terms of deciding whether to send "a priest" to New York. He suggested to Irala the possibility of adding Don Alberto Onaindia to the delegation. Irala applauded the idea, which he supported with reasons and arguments that today, with the perspective supplied by the passage of time, appear highly peculiar. Captivated by the economic, social, and media power he discovered in the United States, Irala attributed to American Catholicism a leading role in the future evolution of the Catholic Church. He judged that a good understanding with U.S. Catholic sectors—a task that Onaindia, a canon, could carry out with aplomb—would be of strategic value for Basque nationalists. Irala had in mind not only the immediate propaganda effect of the delegation's activities in New York, but also its strategic significance with an eye toward the future:

> I say this to you in relation to your question about the advantageousness of Don Alberto Onaindia coming. We had thought about precisely that previously, but we did not say anything to you, since we believed that it would be impossible for him to come, in view of the activity that we supposed it would be necessary for him to be engaged in over there.
>
> We see the question in the following way: from what was said in a conversation with Montavon, we deduce that U.S. Catholics would be thrilled to find a way to change their attitude with regard to the war in Spain. In a not-too-distant future, U.S. Catholicism is going to stand at the head of world Catholicism, due to its prestige, its purity in the midst of others, and its power, both economic and political. Our ability to gain entry at present may be decisive for all time; on the other hand, they agree with us in their social concerns and democratic politics and even in their political inclinations about the formation of states. The Civil War that has separated us up to the present may, and should, become the means that begins to unite us in the future.
>
> Don Alberto's presence can give absolute seriousness to all Basque dealings with the hierarchy and high-ranking circles. He can be the liaison element between the French hierarchy and the hierarchy here, for the purpose I mentioned to you previously. . . .
>
> In view of the role that American Catholics are going to play within the Church in the future, it seems indispensable to us that someone like Don Alberto study the terrain and prepare himself in this way, in order to take perfect and effective action later with regard to Euzkadi's spiritual future, with a modern and realistic sensibility. The occasion is a propitious one.[63]

---

63. Letter from Irala to Aguirre, New York, October 11, 1938, in San Sebastian, *The Basque Archives*, 207.

A few days later, Irala warned the Lehendakari once again that it would be advisable not to increase the delegation's personnel, other than with additions that had been well considered in advance. His arguments, as always, were very reasonable. Haste was not a good counselor: so Irala thought. It was a bad idea to follow one's impulses, because insufficiently considered decisions could have counterproductive effects:

> We unanimously believe that the arrival of Don Alberto could be useful under current circumstances; this is not the case for other elements, unless they were well-known figures in the American world, which we unfortunately do not have among us. The arrival of new Basque representatives now would in our opinion have the following disadvantages: a certain bad impression among the Hispanics and Americans due to the presence of an elevated number of commissioners together. They would interpret it as excessive ostentation. The result of our work would not be in proportion to the number of individuals, above all when it would still be necessary to finish up details of preparation; orienting new arrivals would cause us to lose time that we need to complete initiatives already begun. The financial sacrifice would amount to significant sums.[64]

In the end, Onaindia's transfer did not take place, for reasons that we have not found explicitly stated in writing in the delegation's correspondence, but among which probably figured the fact that he did not speak English and was devoting himself at that time to managing the Exiled Basque Priests' Group (Agrupación de Sacerdotes Vascos Exiliados). This did not mean that the delegation's staff remained immutable, however. Already in December 1938, the Lehendakari was making new appointments: José Urresti and the priest Eustasio de Arritola, both of whom were appointed on December 6,[65] embarked immediately for New York. Urresti's addition to the delegation was followed by the departure of Irala, who returned to Paris in early 1939 in order to take charge of coordinating the Basque government's services abroad from a position in the Lehendakari's general secretariat. He remained there until 1942.

Before embarking for Paris, however, Irala sent the Lehendakari some considerations regarding the delegation's composition that should be men-

---

64. Letter from Irala to Aguirre, New York, November 13, 1938, in San Sebastian, *The Basque Archives*, 217.

65. The credential issued by the general secretary of the President's Office, Pedro Basaldua, referred to them as members "of the North American propaganda delegation of this Presidential Office, directly dependent on the delegate, Don Antonio de Irala."

tioned because they clearly express the difficulties that marked the office's launch. Irala did not express in this letter anything different from what he had suggested in his previous missives, even if in this case he formulated it more bluntly. In his judgment, the delegation was facing "a vital problem" that had to be solved "without losing a minute." The problem was very easy to state: "Simply put, there are too many people, and there's a great deal of expense; we're running out of money." His highly accurate observations were in line with the warnings he had formulated in previous weeks and gave outlet to a veiled criticism of the precipitation with which action had been taken from the President's Office, making decisions and appointments without taking into account his advice and counsel:

> Good old Arritola, a magnificent person, very cultured, cannot do anything with the Basques. This is a problem in which we have to go slowly, and it's not urgent at the moment, especially when there are others to put forward in ecclesiastical circles. In addition, he has a problem with his licenses, he's nervous, he's not a person used to handling affairs, he's off-balance, sighing to go to Chile. In theory, he could do something with the hierarchy; in practice, we believe—it's a unanimous opinion and without any doubt—that it would turn out better if, for example, Urresti did it. A priest like Arritola will be an inferior, and in addition, he'll have to go with an interpreter. In summary, he won't do anything at all, he can't do it, he's not up for it. I've tested him with a task, and nothing.

Irala communicated to the Lehendakari several drastic decisions that, in his judgment, would contribute to alleviating the dysfunction that certain steps taken without sufficient reflection were causing in the delegation's functioning:

> Since your letter had not arrived, and it's an urgent matter, we all agreed to send you the telegram saying that Arritola wants to go to Chile, Aramburu to be independent of the delegation, not being a burden, as he writes, and I to Paris. Since he is useless in practice, I indicated to Aramburu that he should offer to go to Paris. He told me that he would propose to you, by letter and for reasons of his personal situation, that he should be outside the delegation, receive the salary you assigned him, and remain in New York until he resolves some matters that may be of interest to him.[66]

As is evident, the delegation's launch entailed difficulties and unpleasant surprises that were not always easily resolved. The eagerness to launch a

---

66. Letter from Irala to Aguirre, January 31, 1939.

propaganda effort that had produced excellent results in Europe as quickly as possible in the United States led to overly hasty decisions that were not always the right ones. Despite everything, the delegation gradually got underway and launched several lines of action that over the years would turn out to be notably fruitful.

We must not get ahead of our story, however.

Lombana, third from left, with Lehendakari Agirre (fourth from left).

An Ambitious Program of Work

Once established in the city of skyscrapers, New York, Irala and the two Sotas set immediately to work initiating contacts in five directions: with the Basque community resident in the United States, which obviously had to be their first and chief interlocutor; with the American government, which would ultimately be the one to decide the country's position with regard to the civil war in general and the Basque case in particular; with the communications media, always decisive in the success of propaganda endeavors; with U.S. civil society, within which they paid special attention to leading Catholics and Catholic groups; and with ambassadors from other countries accredited there, with the aim of winning the complicity of the diplomatic corps. Clearly, the plan of work was ambitious. It excluded no one who might be relevant, and the task was, precisely for that reason, a gargantuan one. The mission consisted in generating among all these sectors a sympathetic and favorable attitude toward the position adopted by Catholic Basque nationalism in the Spanish Civil War and arousing, to the extent possible, their solidarity, with a view toward collecting funds for their needs.

Relations with the Basque Community in the United States

Contacts with the Basque community began with Valentín Aguirre, a vigorous and very active Basque American born in the foothills of Mount Sollube in Bizkaia, who played a certain preeminent role at the heart of the Basque colony thanks in part to his natural leadership abilities and in part to his comfortable financial position; with the leaders of the Basque Center in New York; and with two well-known Basque nationalists residing in the city, Vidal Mendizábal and Pedro Toja, both from Bermeo (Bizkaia). As Lombana noted in his report, Mendizábal and Toja had already established a Pro-Euzkadi Committee upon the outbreak of the civil war with the objective of raising funds for the Basque government, for which purpose they set up a system of "ongoing and continuous subscription among the Basques" that they were forced to end when President Roosevelt signed the first Neutrality Act in mid-1937.

The first snapshot of the situation, focused exclusively on the Basques residing in New York, showed a panorama more divided than was desirable. The situation was not bad, but it could be improved. The Basque colony was not very large,[67] nor, with a few exceptions, could it be said that its members enjoyed a particularly comfortable financial position. As Lombana stated in his report, it was made up of people of humble origin who "arrived there without support from the classic uncle or family friend." In the majority of cases, they were men who had signed on to merchant ships and, once they arrived in New York, "deserted from the ships on which they were serving." Nevertheless, not everything was negative in this initial evaluation. There was sufficient human material in the United States with which to work toward building a solid Basque colony united around a shared national consciousness.

---

67. "In New York," the first activity report noted, "there are not a large number of Basques; in total, they may be estimated at around four hundred families, which would come to 2,500 or 3,000 souls, including, naturally, the children of Basques born in New York." Quoted in San Sebastian, *The Basque Archives*, 135.

In its first activity report, the delegation[68] noted that the Basque emigrant community in New York was made up in large part of people "originating in the coastal towns of Bizkaia" who "had never been inclined in favor of the Spanish ideologies" that supported Franco and, on the contrary, had received "the Basque patriotic movement" with a fair degree of enthusiasm. Nevertheless, their own errors and the pernicious influence of others had made it impossible to endow the community with a cohesive and committed organization prepared to respond efficiently to the delegation's needs. Irala lamented that "due to personal conflicts and to the poor way in which the specifically Basque movement was channeled, it turned out to be very difficult for the Basques as such to acknowledge the authority that the Euzkadi government should entail for all." It was possible to remain hopeful, however. The delegates were optimistic in this regard, insofar as they came to realize that "the people in general are good, with healthy intentions, *euzkeldunes* [Basque-speakers], and that progress could be made in a short time, avoiding all pretexts for disputes, directing the movement toward a line of action that we could call national."[69]

The Basque New Yorkers responded quite satisfactorily to the delegation's encouragements. Despite past clashes, they gave a unified hearing to its appeals, met several times in an atmosphere of notable enthusiasm, and within their modest economic possibilities, contributed to the collections and subscriptions organized by Irala's team in solidarity with the refugees. In September 1938, in a letter addressed to Lehendakari Aguirre, Irala celebrated the amount of progress that had been made in the effort to see to it that Basques settled in New York would find in the delegation "the binding force of which they were so much in need."[70] At the end of the month, his optimism was even greater. Irala wrote to the Lehendakari that "those in New York are good now. All are with our government; I don't know a single exception."[71] The excellent results obtained in so short a lapse of time made it possible to hold the highest hopes for the future. On this point, the realism that habitually governed the activities of the delegation's members did not prevent them from incorporating a touch of euphoria in their evaluation. The work done had borne its fruits, but the mission had not been exhausted. There was much that could still be done. "In the future,"

---

68. San Sebastián, *The Basque Archives*, 135ff.

69. Ibid., 137.

70. Letter from Irala to Aguirre, New York, September 3, 1938, in ibid., 189.

71. Letter from Irala to Aguirre, New York, September 28, 1938, in ibid., 199.

Irala and his comrades observed, "it will not be difficult to get absolutely all the Basques of New York to behave as such, acting in accordance with a national line."[72] However, the task to be undertaken would not be as easy as they hoped. A year later, the head of the delegation was still reporting to Paris that he continued to work "to see whether I can reconcile our Basques here, for which purpose I went to dine with them yesterday at the Basque Center."[73]

Toward the end of 1938, once their first steps in New York had taken root, the members of the delegation began to extend their activities to the Western states in which there was a notable Basque presence. In California, Nevada, and Idaho, the number of Basques was higher than in the Eastern cities, around forty thousand people. Irala and Manu Sota personally traveled to Idaho, Nevada, Utah, and Oregon. They decided not to visit California, because its enormous territorial extent would not allow them to carry out a minimally effective visit, given the circumstances under which they were working. It was not a population that was very well-off from a financial perspective, but its members lived their Basque identity with great intensity, maintaining Euskara—which they habitually used, passing it down from one generation to the next—and cultivating a large portion of the cultural and folkloric traditions of their place of origin.

Nevertheless, patriotic feelings were not very strong among them, because, given the epoch in which most of them had emigrated, "our compatriots not only left without possessing an elementary education in citizenship, but also without having experienced the Basque renaissance movement in Euzkadi." On the patriotic front, there was much work to be done. As Irala noted, "they are Basques by force of the race, as if by instinct, but national consciousness is lacking [in them], because they know very little about the homeland."[74] Only the most recent immigrants, the members of the delegation observed, "especially the Basques who experienced the national struggle in Euzkadi, retain these concerns and maintain them in full vigor."

In any event, the colony was not hostile to their mission, rather the reverse; the solidity of their Basque identity inclined them in favor of the

---

72. San Sebastián, *The Basque Archives*, 138.

73. Letter from Urresti to Irala, New York, August 23, 1939 (Archivo Iñaki Anasagasti, Fondo Delegación EEUU).

74. Letter from Irala to Aguirre, Boise, December 25, 1938, in San Sebastian, *The Basque Archives*, 234–37.

delegation's messages. According to Irala, "those who appear to be Franco's sympathizers" were "very rare."[75]

The first contact with Basques who had settled in the West took place in December 1938. The Basque government's representatives were welcomed with sympathy and hospitality, "even by some who were judged to be Franco's sympathizers." They succeeded in getting a local newspaper to include a page entirely devoted to the Basque colony, offering a significant propaganda outlet of great potential. The Basques settled in the West responded reasonably well to the events organized for the purpose of raising funds for the refugees in France.

Nevertheless, and contrary to what they had reason to expect, their relationship with the bishop was unfortunate. He received them very curtly and opposed their desire to encourage "two or three little parish priests of ours, who would be zealous, patriotic, and personally winning," to move to that area. Even so, not everything was a disappointment; they could hope. On leaving Boise, Irala once again confirmed that the Basques residing in Idaho "have always remained on the sidelines of any political or patriotic concern," but he affirmed with satisfaction that "we can say that they are all on our side."[76] One man, John Achabal, a native of Ispaster (Bizkaia) and endowed with great natural talents, would serve as a liaison for the launch of a humanitarian project by the Idaho Basques for the benefit of the refugees in France.

In November 1939, Ramón Sota made a new trip, "in a great loop around the United States," in the course of which he would maintain numerous contacts and give lectures in Idaho, Nevada, California, and other Western states.[77] One of the chief tasks facing the delegation in its relations with the Basque diaspora in the United States was the compilation of a census of Basque Americans that would be as complete and exhaustive as possible. The members devoted great effort to compiling a registry in which each Basque in the United States was assigned a card, recording his name, personal information, and address, for the purpose of facilitating potential subsequent contacts. The delegation's correspondence with the staff of President Aguirre's office in Paris is full of "additional" lists of Basques destined to contribute to this census.

---

75. San Sebastián, *The Basque Archives*, 163.

76. Letter from Irala to Aguirre, Boise, December 27, 1938, in ibid., 236.

77. Letter from Manu Sota to Irala, New York, November 7, 1939 (Archivo Iñaki Anasagasti, Fondo Delegación EEUU).

The first news of the delegation's ventures on American soil soon reached Spain, and the reaction of the Falangist Basque press was, as always, aggressive and ferocious. An item in *El Correo Español-El Pueblo Vasco* at the beginning of 1939 recounted the delegation's American tour in what were hardly the most respectful of terms:

> the Basque nationalists, breast-beating Catholics of zero morality, have come up with the pretext that [funds collected to aid their refugees resident in France and in Red Spain] come from subscriptions by the Basques residing in California. It is an odd coincidence, however, that the Basques residing in California who have returned to Europe have all entered Spain declaring themselves supporters of Franco, since they are modest laborers ignorant of English, speaking only Basque, who over the years, by labor and privation, working as shepherds in the Far West, have succeeded in saving up a small capital that they are not disposed to turn over to politicians of such ramshackle morality.
>
> Understanding that their chosen justification can be accepted only by those unfamiliar with the true economic situation of the Basques of California, the separatist leaders turned to those who reside in New York, asking them to send their donations to the Euzkadi government instead of to the CGT [the Confederación General del Trabajo or General Confederation of Labor, an anarcho-syndicalist labor union in Spain], but since the majority are longshoremen with anarchist ideas, they refused to go along, blowing a hole in the planned farce.[78]

Relations with American Society

At the beginning of September 1938, Irala wrote to the Lehendakari, mentioning some of the contacts he was developing with "the Americans, especially with a view toward an organization providing financial aid to Euzkadi."[79] The chief social group targeted by the delegation in its activities, at least in its first phase, was logically that of the Catholics. The Lehendakari communicated as much to the Republic's ambassador in Washington, D.C., and that was the program of work they followed.

The Republic's diplomatic representation in the United States considered this choice a correct one and made no objections to their work. On the contrary, the consul-general in New York confessed to Manu Sota that

---

78. "Especulaciones: A que se dedican ahora los dirigentes vascos," *El Correo Español: El Pueblo Vasco,* January 10, 1939.

79. Letter from Irala to Aguirre, New York, September 10, 1938, in San Sebastian, *The Basque Archives,* 192.

he was "very interested" in that work, because propaganda directed to the Catholic world was "the most difficult, most important, and most effective" in which they could engage. In addition, it was among Catholics that the credential letters brought by the delegation members, all graduates of Jesuit schools and practicing believers with a notable history of Catholic activism, could have the greatest effect. They said as much in their first joint meeting. The Republic's diplomats stationed in New York understood the Basque delegation's activities as an ideal complement to the work they were engaged in: "they believe," Irala wrote in his notebook, "that due to our status as Basque Catholics, known by all the world, we can enter circles that would be closed to them."[80]

The difficulties were evident, however. By 1938, the American Catholic population had to a large extent already taken a position regarding the Spanish Civil War, and as we have seen in the preceding sections, positions critical of the Republic and favorable to Franco were prevalent in their written media. As Manu Sota would write years later, recalling this period, "in no country in the world have the Catholics risen up more decidedly in favor of Franco's cause."[81] Not by chance, the president of the American Civil Liberties Union, Roger Baldwin, warned them immediately upon their arrival that, despite everything, "their worst enemy would be the Catholic Church"; he was not wrong. In their relations with the chief U.S. Catholic sectors, the members of the delegation experienced moments of intense powerlessness and frustration. Two episodes can serve as examples. In 1939, a year after disembarking in New York and making countless contacts with the Catholic sector of society, Manu Sota's distrust of U.S. Catholics was manifest. In a letter sent to Paris, he observed that "as far as American Catholics are concerned, I adopt the attitude of St. Thomas, 'seeing is believing.' There's no one who outdoes them in fine words, but when it comes to deeds, they make a long face [*hacen mirri*]."[82] A year later, in 1940, Manu Sota himself drew up a report on the position of U.S. Catholics "in the European war," in which he included some openly critical evaluations of a quite extremist, fanatical, and clerical community, made up fundamentally of "Irish, who are followed in importance by the Italians,

80. Note dated September 18, 1938, in ibid., 79.

81. Analysis of the position of the Catholics of the United States in relation to the European war, New York, May 7, 1940 (Archivo Iñaki Anasagasti, Fondo Delegación EEUU), 2.

82. Letter from Manu Sota to Irala, New York, November 6, 1939 (Archivo Iñaki Anasagasti, Fondo Delegación EEUU).

the Spanish-speakers, the Poles, the Czechs, etc."[83] With mordant sarcasm, behind which can be glimpsed the frustrations accumulated in years dedicated to seeking the support of American Catholics, Sota noted that the best way to influence them "is not working in the United States, but in tiny Vatican City." It is useless, he added, to aspire to influence "the ideology of these twenty-one million Catholics, who blindly follow the orders of their bishops (even if they occasionally understand that they are wrong), while the latter follow the dictates of Rome."[84] Convincing the average American Catholic, Sota observed, turned out to be very difficult, because he did not pay attention to logical argument. "The American," he added,

> is a very independent being, but if he is Catholic, he turns over the rudder that is to set his religious course to the first ecclesiastic who takes charge of the administration of his soul, and he will blindly obey his commands, which encompass a very wide scope, since it is well-known that religion may be connected with everything. In the same way, the ecclesiastic will follow the instructions he receives from the hierarchy, from which he will not diverge for an instant. This religious discipline becomes more visible in the United

---

83. Analysis of the position of the Catholics of the United States in relation to the European war, New York, May 7, 1940 (Archivo Iñaki Anasagasti, Fondo Delegación EEUU), 1. His comments are particularly harsh and cutting with regard to the Irish, about whom he says that, "intriguers and unscrupulous by nature, they pull the strings of the destinies of the Catholic Church in this country, at the same time that they are very involved in political life. This has the result that the influence of the Irish and of the Catholic Church is very large in the United States, in the religious, political, and social arenas" (p. 2). Further on, he adds, "The Irish of the United States are, in the majority, poor people and of a very low cultural level, easily tricked, especially by the clergy, whom they believe and obey without question [*a pies juntillas*]. Out of the fifteen million unemployed in these states, a large proportion are Irish Catholics, and also Italian Catholics, although a smaller number. They are, therefore, fertile soil for any extremist seed. Their poverty and religiosity make them susceptible to political-religious movements of the type led by Father Coughlin and his followers of the Christian Front, who are in favor of direct action to attain the totalitarian ends they propose to reach. The Irish, immigrants and children of immigrants defeated by life, are assiduous readers of the *Brooklyn Tablet, Social Justice,* and the rest of the Catholic publications of militant style and extremist ideology. They are the desperate Catholics who find satisfaction for their longings for revenge in the subversive theories preached by those weeklies. They are more Roman Catholics than Apostolic ones, and they feel their not-very-Christian impulses justified by the theories maintained by those publications, Catholic to the hilt, always predisposed to forget Christ in order to follow any possessed man who, on the pretext of exterminating communism, murders and imprisons all those who do not worship at the altar of [*no comulguen con*] his anti-democratic ideas. Thanks to this reading, they have learned to hate the Jew, whom they believe to be the cause of all their tragedies, and they justify, up to a certain point, Hitler's repression of the Israelite race, which they consider a bulwark of communism, freemasonry, and liberalism" (p. 3).

84. Ibid., 13.

States due to the fact that the Irish, who are fanatical in the extreme, are the ones who provide the model for American Catholicism.[85]

Nevertheless, the preference given to these sectors in their propaganda work did not mean that the delegation neglected the non-Catholic world. On the contrary, rather, they also engaged in a notable level of activity beyond the Catholic community, although they did not always find among their interlocutors an appropriate channel for making progress in their propaganda effort. For example, soon after the delegation began its activities, they met with Dr. H. Raissig, a Methodist minister who served as general secretary of the North American Committee to Aid Spanish Democracy. Raissig offered his services to help them make contacts with prominent figures in the Catholic world, but he explained that they would be ill advised to be too closely associated with him and his circle, "since they had a reputation as leftists."[86] They also made contact with Roger Baldwin of the American Civil Liberties Union, who thanked them for their visit and the information they provided him, adding that they should "have been working in America for some time already."

In their work with the Catholic world, Irala and his colleagues began with those whom they supposed to be closest to the delegation's positions. As they indicated at the beginning of November 1938, in a letter addressed to Aguirre, they had designed a progressive strategy that would enable them to gradually penetrate the complicated world of American Catholicism: "We are following the guideline of building relationships with Catholics who are of interest and in some way 'easy,' in order to continue studying the terrain, leaving the difficult ones and the hierarchy until we have the letters from [French Cardinal Jean] Verdier, etc., with the aim of acting with the greatest possible safeguards and avoiding a stumble."[87]

A review of the contacts they made with representatives of the Catholic world during their first few months makes it possible to appreciate the rapidity with which they gained access to some of the most prominent shapers of opinion in the Catholic sphere. Certainly, it must be acknowledged that they knew how to maneuver with agility and effectiveness, and it is of great interest to note their evaluations of the people and media out-

---

85. Ibid., 15.

86. Note dated September 9, 1938, in San Sebastián, *The Basque Archives*, 89.

87. Letter from Irala to Aguirre, New York, November 8, 1938, in ibid., 216.

lets with which they made contact, even with a view toward filling out the internal history of American Catholicism during this period.

One of the first shapers of opinion with which they had to make contact was the magazine The *Commonweal*, which, as we have seen, was one of the more balanced press observers of the Spanish civil conflict within the American Catholic world.[88] After various efforts, they succeeded in arranging a meeting with its editor, H. L. Binsse, which took place on September 28, 1938. The members of the delegation recorded in their notes that Binsse was a "pleasant, intelligent, and disheveled [*arlote*]" man, adding that "it is quickly evident that he is a decided anti-fascist."[89] Days later, Irala wrote to Aguirre indicating that "his attitude is much more radically anti-Franco than appears in the magazine; this is due to reasons of prudence with an eye toward other Catholic sectors."

Binsse welcomed them cordially and gave them facilities of all kinds for communicating with U.S. Catholics, including the hierarchy. When they spoke to him about the Basque refugees, he promised to write an editorial for the magazine, making an appeal to the solidarity of U.S. Catholics. Binsse also made a proposal that Irala found excellent; he offered to publish an appeal to American Catholics on behalf of the Basque refugees, on the basis of a letter from the French Catholic committee that was working along these lines. Irala was of the opinion that, if well organized, the initiative might serve to "get a great deal of money."[90] In order for it to succeed, however, it was indispensable to involve the French hierarchy, or at least those of its members who had proved themselves "friends" of Basque Catholic nationalism, such as the bishop of Dax, Cardinal Verdier, etc. That was, as he understood it, the most effective way to enter "into U.S. Catholic terrain fully and by a secure path."[91] In the following weeks, the members of the delegation discussed this plan extensively and exchanged impressions with the Lehendakari by letter.

---

88. Manu Sota observed that The *Commonweal* was "the Catholic publication of the greatest intellectual value in the United States," although he lamented the fact that "its number of readers and its economic prosperity are [not] at the level of its worth," Analysis of the position of the Catholics of the United States in relation to the European war, New York, May 7, 1940 (Archivo Iñaki Anasagasti, Fondo Delegación EEUU), 14.

89. Note dated September 28, 1938, in San Sebastián, *The Basque Archives*, 107.

90. Letter from Irala to Aguirre, September 29, 1938, in ibid., 202.

91. Letter from Irala to Aguirre, New York, October 11, 1938, in ibid., 205–7.

With a view toward implementing this initiative, Irala and his fellow representatives seriously considered the possibility of reinforcing their office with additional personnel. The Lehendakari, who had already mentioned his plan of including "a priest" in the delegation in his letter to Fernando de los Ríos in mid-August 1938, evaluated the possibility of sending Canon Alberto Onaindia to New York. Onaindia had been very effective in his efforts among European Catholic circles, especially in France and Italy, and no one doubted that he would be able to do excellent work in the United States. At the delegation, they applauded the idea, but they wrote to Aguirre advising him that, "in order to prevent a stumbling block from Franco's supporters, who will try to go after him," he should come backed by a letter of introduction from Cardinal Verdier introducing him to the hierarchy, or at least a letter for Cardinal Mundelein describing his mission as "informational."[92]

Various strategies for organizing the Catholic Committee were discussed. The complicity of the Irish, perhaps more inclined to understand the specificity of the Basque problem, seemed to point toward interesting possibilities. Irala wrote to the Lehendakari indicating that "we may be of interest to the Irish Catholic sector, since we are Catholics and have a national problem."[93] Frank P. Walsh offered his services to that end. He was an Irish Catholic, a friend of Roosevelt, and a former leader of the Irish working in the United States for Irish independence, and he enjoyed prestige and access.

As time passed, the delegation became increasingly persuaded that the Catholic platform, beyond its intrinsic value, could be of great help in naturalizing their message in American society. "The Catholics," Irala wrote to Aguirre, "are the arbiters of the presidential election, and for that reason they exercise so much influence on his [President Roosevelt's] decisions."[94] According to the head of the delegation, the plan to be followed was as follows:

1. See to it that the "unconditional humanitarian disposition of certain Catholic sectors in favor of the Basques spreads or at least acquires general resonance." For this purpose, the presence of

---

92. Ibid., 206.

93. Letter from Irala to Aguirre, New York, October 15, 1938, in ibid., 208.

94. Letter from Irala to Aguirre, New York, October 21, 1938, in ibid., 211.

Alberto Onaindia with the French hierarchy's endorsement could be of great value.

2. Work to obtain a declaration, "if not by the hierarchy, then by prominent Catholics, many of whom are wishing for it, in favor of peace in Spain, an end to hatred, and the defense of co-existence." The declaration would be based on principles such as the defense of individual freedom, respect for religious conscience, and respect for ideological and ethnic minorities as guarantees of their legal recognition.

With these credentials, it would be easier to approach the president of the republic. On this point, Irala's reflections were categorical: "backing from the Catholics, however few they may be, is a decisive element for the president, especially in Spanish affairs."

At the beginning of November 1938, the credential letter from Cardinal Verdier arrived at the delegation, where, Irala confessed, "it comes in very useful for us, in order to start working among the Catholics."[95] Shortly afterward, other letters arrived, from the archbishop of Bordeaux and the bishop of Dax. To Irala, they seemed "very handsome," and he trusted that they would have "a great effect among American Catholics."[96]

Efforts to establish a Basque Aid Committee began immediately. In late December 1938, Ramón Sota visited the editor of *The Commonweal*, Philip Burnham, to present him with a plan brought from Euskadi by Urresti. The plan was to evacuate Basque children to Catalonia; the effort was evaluated very positively.

They also contacted Montavon, a layman and legal advisor to the National Catholic Welfare Conference and the intellectual inspiration for a large share of the more flexible positions defended within the American Catholic community in relation to the civil war. He was a man of great influence in the American Catholic world, with close contacts at the Vatican. He was familiar with Spain, where he had traveled in the time of the Republic, and he was well informed about the evolution of events in the war. He had a good command of Spanish, which facilitated his access to available information about the conflict. He was reasonably well informed and no stranger to the Basque problem. He was familiar with the general

---

95. Letter from Irala to Aguirre, New York, November 13, 1938, in ibid., 219.

96. Letter from Irala to Aguirre, Boise, December 19, 1938, in ibid., 229.

outlines of what had been discussed in the international media as "the Basque case."

Montavon had been the author of a pamphlet titled *Insurrection in Spain,* a pioneer among American Catholic publications about the Spanish Civil War and quite balanced in its distribution of blame and responsibility, although overly simplistic in its analysis and evaluation of certain events. Evidence of his circumspection was the affirmation that a military defeat inflicted by either of the contending parties on the other would never bring "lasting peace to Spain," in which he wished to see a democratic and representative government that would respect fundamental rights and ensure a just peace for all. It was one of the few texts that, coming from activist Catholic pens, did not end up taking a position clearly in favor of Franco. Many, who had ingenuously pinned all their hopes on Franco's ability to organize a civilized coexistence, would not open their eyes until years later, when World War II revealed the deep fascist roots of his regime for the entire world to see.

Incredible though it may seem, in 1938, many Catholics only saw Franco as a man motivated by the firm determination to restore religious freedom in the framework of a free, just, democratic regime respectful of fundamental rights, cutting off at the root the dangers of a communism as aggressive as it was tenacious. Montavon developed an interesting complicity with the members of the Basque delegation. They met with him on September 24 and 26, 1938, in two meetings in which they were able to confirm that he possessed solid and very carefully considered views about what had happened in the war. He did not believe in the legitimacy of Franco's movement, and he considered the collective letter promoted by Gomá to have been imprudent at best. He did not trust Franco, but neither would he criticize him openly, because he did not want to (and should not) open a breach in American Catholicism.

Sometime later, Irala reiterated his initial impressions (cited above), observing that "this gentleman is considerate toward us and wants to find out about things." Montavon was an important backer of the delegation and its position. He was a great help in its mission. That was how Irala saw it when he wrote that "through Montavon, we can work a great deal, and surely with results."[97]

---

97. Letter from Irala to Aguirre, New York, November 2, 1938, in ibid., 215.

On November 12, 1938, Irala went to visit him in Washington, D.C., with Verdier's letter endorsing the project of forming an aid committee for the Basque refugees. Once again, he received an excellent welcome. As Irala wrote to the Lehendakari, "that gentleman cannot be better, at least in words; we should try to see everything carried out. Up to now, he has given us evidence of affection and trust, and we have no right to think that it will not be that way going forward."[98]

The delegation continued to maintain contact with Montavon and regularly informed him about the evolution of events in Spain. Soon after the conclusion of the civil war, Irala sent him from Paris a complete report on the situation of the Basque refugees in southern France. By return mail, Montavon thanked him for sending it, adding some reflections that show the ingenuousness with which in U.S. Catholic sectors, even people less intoxicated by Falangist propaganda thought about what could be expected from the Spanish dictator once he had won the war:

> That those fifty-nine thousand refugees should return to Spain is evident. Not all of them, because there will be those who might face charges for their political activities. There will also be those who might face serious criminal charges. It can be presumed, however, that a considerable majority of the adults, and all the children and the majority of the women, have not committed any offense.
>
> Do you believe that an appeal by the leaders of the Basque People requesting clemency, on the basis of an acknowledgement of error in their political conduct and reaffirmed with a firm intention of remaining loyal under the government of National Spain, would be possible? And in that case, what do you believe that General Franco's reaction would be?[99]

In this excellent and unruffled relationship, there was only one discordant note. In late 1939, Manu Sota received a confidential report that Montavon, the legal secretary of the National Catholic Welfare Conference, had betrayed his trust. According to this report, Montavon had told the bishop of Texas that the members of the delegation were untrustworthy because they were engaged in a "campaign against the Spanish hierarchy," an accusation that led the prelate to refuse to support the League of Friends of the Basques and to try to convince the other bishops to do the same. Sota was enraged and wrote a furious letter to Paris in which the worst of

---

98. Letter from Irala to Aguirre, New York, November 13, 1938, in ibid., 217.

99. Letter from Montavon to Irala, undated, but from late April 1939 (Archivo Iñaki Anasagasti, Fondo Delegación EEUU).

epithets, starting with that of "satrap," were reserved for Montavon. The missive included a certain reproach to Irala for having trusted too much in this leader of American Catholic opinion. All the same, when evaluating Manu Sota's letters, the human factor should not be lost from view. In Sota's judgment of Montavon, and in his judgment of the American Catholic elites in general, his passionate personality and his notable inclination to vehemence and creativity cannot be overlooked. Definitively, Manu was not going through a good period:

> The rascality of Montavon, always so friendly toward us, is clearly evident. He asks us for testimony about the Spanish hierarchy (and he asks us for it with a great deal of interest), we send it to him confidentially, and then he says that we are campaigning against the hierarchy . . . We've asked Montavon to explain to us the scope of that report he sent to the bishops telling them that we are campaigning against the hierarchy. We'll see what he answers. We're ready to handle the matter entirely diplomatically, but if this doesn't get a result, we'll appeal to whomever it takes and show our hand, and then we'll see who comes off badly. They'll say that Montavon is in the right (they say the same about Franco and almost about Hitler), but he'll come out of the scuffle with a loss of prestige. You'll be convinced that the Catholic bosses here are repugnantly lacking in morality. In the current war also, they're playing Hitler's game, and they don't dare to declare themselves fascists because they're afraid of public opinion, but that is what they are on the sly, which is what is most dangerous.[100]

Another Catholic leader with whom they made contact was Michael J. Ready, an Irish nationalist and the general secretary of the National Catholic Welfare Conference. Curiously, they did not find him to be overly interested in the problem of Spain, although, after a long interview, he concluded by observing that the Basque problem "was the same as that of Ireland,"[101] a comment that gave hope to the members of the delegation.

They also expressed their satisfaction at their contacts with those in charge of the other magazine that, along with *The Commonweal*, had shown greater sympathy for the republican cause in the civil war. This was the *Catholic Worker*, a weekly publication strongly committed to defending and spreading the Church's social teachings.[102]

---

100. Letter from Manu Sota to Irala, New York, November 27, 1939 (Archivo Iñaki Anasagasti, Fondo Delegación EEUU).

101. Note dated September 26, 1938, in San Sebastián, *The Basque Archives*, 105.

102. As Manu Sota observed, it was a weekly published by a group of Christian idealists, seeking to counteract radical currents among the working class with articles based on the papal

On October 27, 1938, they met with the *Catholic* Worker's director, Mr. Callahan, and several members of the staff. On the occasion of this first meeting, they could happily confirm that "they are rabid opponents of Franco, they realize the danger that the Church is facing in Spain, and they are deeply concerned about it." They were very interested in the Basque issue, because what had happened with the nationalist Catholics could be a topic of great interest with a view toward promoting their ideas in the face of the monolithic, idolatrous support of Franco that prevailed among U.S. Catholics. They offered help and support, of course, but they asked for endorsements from the French hierarchy in order to defend themselves against possible attacks.

The delegation's contacts were not limited to those Catholic circles friendliest to their position, however. Even earlier than was planned under the progressive strategy about which Irala wrote to the Lehendakari in his letters, they also approached some of those who had opposed their position most belligerently. They even met with the Jesuit Talbot, who, as we have seen, was the author and promoter of the most intransigent positions in opposition to the pro-republican fighters. The Basque nationalists were perfectly familiar with Talbot's work and the positions that the U.S. Jesuit had been adopting with regard to the Spanish Civil War. Their perception of him can be summarized in this phrase included by Irala in one of the numerous letters he sent to the Lehendakari from the New York delegation: "He is an authentic ambassador for Franco."

However, Talbot and his magazine, *America*, exercised enormous influence in the Catholic world, and not only in the United States. What was published in the American periodical was followed with interest even at the Vatican itself. Evidence of this is what Father Goenaga, stationed in Rome, wrote to Felipe Urkola[103] in a letter dated November 1938. Goenaga warned Urkola about the contents of an article signed by Connolly and published in the October 22 issue of *America*. The article, as the cleric explained, aimed to give the lie to "Maritain and his disciples" by describing the reality of National Spain as it really was. With regard to the Basques,

---

encyclicals. "They are true Christians," he noted, "and the sympathetic position they adopted during the Spanish war was heavily attacked by the Catholics who supported Franco." Analysis of the position of the Catholics of the United States in relation to the European war, New York, May 7, 1940 (Archivo Iñaki Anasagasti, Fondo Delegación EEUU), 13.

103. Felipe Urkola was a journalist stationed at the Basque delegation in Paris, occupied along with the head of the delegation in publishing the newspaper *Euzko Deya*.

the article was ironic, affirming that "suddenly, the Basque region discovered its unique racial history and demanded to govern itself." The religious orders, however, according to Connolly, proclaimed the need for unity and educated the youth and the labor unions in this principle. "Consequently, the National Movement acquired the character of Saint George attacking the two-headed monster of separatism and apathy." In that pursuit, it attacked the Basques with the same harshness with which it fought communism. Disgusted, and to a certain degree alarmed, Goenaga summarized the contents of the publication, with special attention to what it affirmed with regard to the Basques, and he observed in his letter to Urkola, "Have you read the October 22 issue of the *America* weekly in the USA? . . . Of course, some better things were also written in that article. There's only a page on the Basques."[104] The initiative came from the priest himself, who saw to it that the members of the delegation were informed of his desire for an interview. The latter, of course, agreed to the request. The meeting took place on the afternoon of September 20, 1938. It was attended by the three members of the delegation, prepared to deploy all their dialectical capabilities in the conversation.

Once it was over, Irala viewed the interview with interest, not so much because they had convinced him, a difficult endeavor, if not an impossible one, but because "he heard truths, which always make an impression and produce an effect." The letter Irala sent to the Lehendakari included several sequences of images worthy of reproduction in a movie script:

> In addition to what is said in a case like this, there is something else that remains behind and is in the air. You would have to have seen a man like Father Talbot flustered by the presence of three 'chumps' ['*coitaos*'] and starting the conversation by saying that he has nothing against the Basques, that he is a friend, that he has received a letter from Rome telling him about the truth of our position, etc. That between Barcelona and Franco, he'll take Franco; that is, he said, his position. We began by kissing his hand, like the perfect disciples of the Jesuits that we are, and then speaking slowly and smoothly. When the name of Aguirre came up, he appeared to shudder; he couldn't help it.
>
> Of course, he was impressed, and he'll take good care not to speak against the Basques. We'll also take good care to send him all our things, with true

---

104. Letter from Goenaga to Urkola, Rome, November 3, 1938 (Archivo Iñaki Anasagasti, Fondo Delegación EEUU). In Basque in original, translated by Cameron J. Watson.

importunity, and keep alert for whether he wants to pull some trick on us, since anything is possible. He fears us; that's beyond doubt.[105]

The case of the Basque Catholics, which the EAJ-PNV and Aguirre's government itself had publicized as the most absolute rebuttal of Franco's endeavor to convert the war into a crusade, had a prominent role in the American political debate about the Spanish Civil War. There were many who, especially after the bombing of Gernika in April 1937, cited it in order to identify the correct perspective on the conflict. We have already seen the displeasure this produced in Cárdenas.

The magazine *America,* however, which Talbot directed, repeatedly dismissed the ethical relevance of the Basque case, denying that it had anything to do with religion. On this and other points, Talbot was prey to Franco's propaganda. In the view of the members of the Basque delegation, "he knows a fair amount about the Basque nationalist problem, but he is completely unfamiliar with the spirit that exists in Spain in opposition to this nationalism." Perhaps because he was unaware of this point, he told the Basque nationalists that it was in their interest to build a rapprochement with Franco, "since in the end, with a civilian government, we would be given freedoms; also because Franco is more likely to win."[106] The meeting was not particularly fruitful—they were meeting with a man who mimicked the rebels so closely that he even affirmed that "all those who oppose Franco are undoubtedly Reds"[107]—but neither was it entirely negative. Irala viewed him as "one of the most intelligent Jesuits I have met"[108] and left with the feeling that it was worth the trouble to continue sending him letters and reports that would serve to contrast with and/or to complete his habitual sources of information, unfailingly located in Franco's orbit. Talbot, do not forget, had been characterized by the members of the delegation as a "true ambassador of Franco."

---

105. Letter from Irala to Aguirre, New York, September 21, 1938, in San Sebastian, *The Basque Archives*, 196.

106. Note dated September 20, 1938, in ibid., 102.

107. Analysis of the position of the Catholics of the United States in relation to the European war, New York, May 7, 1940 (Archivo Iñaki Anasagasti, Fondo Delegación EEUU), 4.

108. A bit more of an iconoclast, Manu Sota said of him that he was "a man who hides his lack of culture under the cloak of his fanaticism and industriousness." Cf. Analysis of the position of the Catholics of the United States in relation to the European war, New York, May 7, 1940 (Archivo Iñaki Anasagasti, Fondo Delegación EEUU), 3.

The following year, with the civil war over, Manuel Inchausti proposed visiting him again, to seek his collaboration and support for the International League of Friends of the Basques (Liga Internacional de Amigos de los Vascos, LIAV), which he was trying to establish in the United States following the French model. American Catholic endorsement was essential if the effort was to succeed. Like the members of the delegation, Inchausti thought that "if what is wanted is that the League not end up grouped and catalogued among the other Spanish organizations here, it is necessary at any cost to win the cooperation and adhesion of the Catholics first,"[109] and among American Catholics, Talbot and his weekly *America* constituted an extraordinarily important node of influence.

At the end of August 1939, the proposal was put forward to hold an exploratory interview with him, "without presenting the matter to him, but solely to see whether he has evolved since you visited him."[110] First, however, a conversation was held with Father La Farge, a contributor to and associate editor of the same magazine, "as a first step" toward approaching Talbot.[111] The interview was not much help, however. Inchausti explained to La Farge their plan to create "something similar to the French League," asking for *America*'s collaboration, but La Farge was clear and categorical: "as Father Talbot had already traced out a path of complete agreement with Franco's ideas, as far as the Iberian Peninsula was concerned, and a great deal of money had been spent on propaganda, he believed that it was impossible for the weekly *America* to do anything along these lines."[112]

Despite everything, Inchausti insisted. His tenacity would not allow him to accept defeat in the first exchange, and he asked whether they would permit him to publish an article in his name about the Basques. La Farge agreed, but without too much conviction, because "in the end, it was Father Talbot who would decide." In the end, he recommended that they turn to the weekly *The Commonweal*, a very revealing observation.

---

109. Letter from Inchausti to Aguirre, New York, November 29, 1939. Cf. Jean-Claude Larronde, *Manuel de Ynchausti (1900–1961). Etorri handiko mezenas bat: Un mecenas inspirado*, Basque trans. Susana Preboste Iraizoz (Milafranca-Villefranque: Bidasoa Historia Garaikideko Erakundea, 1998), 103.

110. Letter from Urresti to Irala, New York, August 23, 1939 (Archivo Iñaki Anasagasti, Fondo Delegación EEUU).

111. Letter from Urresti to Irala, New York, August 29, 1939 (Archivo Iñaki Anasagasti, Fondo Delegación EEUU).

112. Letter from Urresti to Irala, New York, October 2, 1939 (Archivo Iñaki Anasagasti, Fondo Delegación EEUU).

In a subsequent letter, however, Urresti included some additional detail with regard to the reasons that led Talbot to maintain an attitude so little disposed to any flexibility in his positions regarding the role played by the Basque nationalists in the civil war. "Although he is convinced," Urresti noted, "of the truth of the facts, he does not want to reverse himself, since he has engaged in so much propaganda along those lines and is afraid of losing prestige with public opinion if he has to unsay everything that he has been publishing up to now."

This judgment, based on information transmitted by Father La Farge himself, is highly significant when it comes to evaluating the delegation's work. Following the first interview with Talbot, Irala wrote to the Lehenda-kari declaring that "he fears us; that's beyond doubt." After that meeting, the members of the delegation were left with the impression that, as far as his positions regarding the Basque case were concerned, the giant Talbot was actually flawed. His outer intransigence hid great internal weakness. Talbot was aware of the scant degree of consistency entailed in some of his positions and was uncomfortable putting forward a radical defense of Falangist ideas in front of a delegation of Catholic Basque nationalists who explained their behavior with humility and supported by firm Gospel foundations. Talbot could not change his positions, however, nor even nuance them. His prestige prevented him, an ill-understood prestige that associated a good name with infallibility.

In late 1939, Manuel de Inchausti continued in the struggle, trying to win Talbot over and attract him toward the International League of Friends of the Basques, with the intermediate step of a reformulation of *America*'s informational line, including news and opinions more favorable to the attitude adopted by "the Basques" in the civil war. In his ironic and iconoclastic style, Manu Sota recounted these efforts to Irala, expressing his skepticism with regard to this line of work. In his opinion, there was no reason to hope for too much from Talbot and his circle:

> Now [Inchausti] is pursuing a monstrous battle against Father Talbot, like Don Quixote against those giants that were no more than windmills. Don Manuel also believes that his fight is with knights and gentlemen, but he has now realized that they are a group of hypocritical and unscrupulous windmills, incapable of milling even a fraction of an ounce of Christian flour.

He is now in a very interesting dispute with *America*. This magazine published a thoroughly irresponsible interview with Father Otano, with the promise that this would serve to allow us Basques to write some open letters that would be published, with the aim of setting up a peaceful polemic that would clarify the Basques' actual position. Father La Farge made us this solemn promise, the corrections that he judged pertinent were made, and he agreed to publish it in last week's issue, but the letter has not been published.

For his part, Ramón sent his letter to Talbot. This did get a reply, but saying that he was not going to publish the letter and affirming that they published the Otano interview in *America* taking advantage of his time in New York, which is incorrect. As a result, Don Manuel is highly indignant and is going to go to the Jesuit superiors, with whom his stock is high. I foresee a triumph for Don Manuel, although he has to deal with scoundrels in cassocks, who are the most dangerous of all the fauna of Artful Dodgers [*rinconetes y cortadillos*].[113]

Irala wrote back to him from Paris, propping up his spirits. At a moment burdened by evil omens, he wanted to infuse optimism and not fail to recognize the positive side of what was happening, and the "tussles" with the Catholic elites were not necessarily negative. With tenacity and effort, the differences could be resolved, and without doubt, they would end up being resolved in a way that was positive for Basque interests. Irala had a cooler head than Manu Sota and was more objective and less impassioned:

I find it interesting what you tell me in your letter about the tussles that good old Don Manuel [Inchausti] is engaged in with Father Talbot and our most dear friend Montavon. I believe that the mere fact that these problems occur is a triumph for us. In these circumstances, that means a great deal. In addition, since they're the ones who are always recalcitrant, it's a question of not leaving them in peace, day after day, with the aim of wearing them down. In this way, without giving way for a minute, when better times come, as they will come, we'll find them much more favorable than if all these incidents hadn't taken place, such that, dear Manu, don't cease targeting them, since even if it's only out of boredom, we'll have to tire them out. In addition, we have to demonstrate to them that they aren't any more stubborn than we are. Also, the fact that more than one bishop has answered in a friendly tone is a great success, don't you think?[114]

---

113. Letter from Manu Sota to Irala, November 27, 1939 (Archivo Iñaki Anasagasti, Fondo Delegación EEUU).

114. Letter from Irala to Manu Sota, Paris, December 12, 1939 (Archivo Iñaki Anasagasti, Fondo Delegación EEUU).

But Talbot was very much Talbot. He was not a man who was easy to persuade or inclined to let himself be convinced, and his deep-rooted pro-Franco convictions were scarcely shaken by Inchausti's assault. That the Basques' efforts did not bear fruit is evident in this furious critique leveled at him by Manu Sota in 1940, upon examining the position of American Catholics with regard to World War II:

> Father Talbot [is a] fanatical and intransigent man, of a reactionary Catholicism, who when he is attacking (and that is his favorite position) often forgets that he is a Christian. *America* is one of so many publications of lamentable ideology that are published with the funds of the Society of Jesus around the world. During the war in Spain, this magazine was the mouthpiece of the military uprising, and there was no outrage by Franco that did not deserve its approval, nor any slander that it was forbidden to hurl against the government's supporters. For Father Talbot, those who fought under Franco's banner (including Nazis and Moors) were the glorious soldiers of Christ, defenders of the faith and of civilization, et cetera. According to him, all Catholics were bound to assist Franco's triumph. Today, for reasons that would be incomprehensible to us if we were not talking about Jesuits, they have become advocates of the most puritanical pacifism, out of Christian conviction. Catholics should remain on the sidelines of this war—they affirm now—but one suspects that Father Talbot would toss his biretta into the air three times if this conflict were won by fascist nations.[115]

Propaganda

From the outset, the members of the delegation began to explore the possibility of publishing in English books and pamphlets on the "Basque case" that had been successfully published in France. We have already seen that among Aguirre's plans for the propaganda work to be done in the United States, a prominent place was held by "the immediate publication of works that here, in Europe, have made a deep impression and attracted abundant critical attention."[116] Very soon, however, they had occasion to confirm the difficulties entailed in a publishing enterprise of that kind. The American reading public bore little resemblance to its European counterpart. Its tastes and inclinations were very different, and it did not appear possible

---

115. Analysis of the position of the Catholics of the United States in relation to the European war, New York, May 7, 1940 (Archivo Iñaki Anasagasti, Fondo Delegación EEUU), 9–10.

116. Letter from Aguirre to Fernando de los Ríos, Paris, August 12, 1938 (Archivo Iñaki Anasagasti, Fondo Delegación EEUU).

to introduce into the transatlantic publishing market everything that had been well received on the other side of the ocean.

As Irala observed in one of his first letters to the Lehendakari, when it came to publishing books in the United States, there were two basic difficulties: "they are little read, and they are extraordinarily expensive."[117] For this reason, the delegation's activity report highlighted the difficulty in interesting a publishing house.

The group that formed the delegation traveled to New York with all the books and pamphlets on the Basques and the civil war that had been published in Europe. Among them all, George Steer's book, originally written in English under the title *The Tree of Guernica*, was the one that offered the greatest possibilities with a view toward the American propaganda challenge. Irala confirmed that "everyone tells us that it would work best as propaganda for our cause." The delegation made various efforts toward arranging its publication, both with the author and with the British publisher to which he had ceded exclusive publication rights. Already in the interview they held in August 1938 with Thomas Davin, a liberal Catholic sent to them by Jay Allen, they heard that "the most interesting" among the publications they wished to introduce into the American market was Steer's book. As far as the other books were concerned, he predicted that "they will scarcely be read," and he argued as follows, affirming that "Writing for the French is different from writing for the Americans and the English. Steer's book, on the other hand, is splendidly well written by someone who knows English and American mentalities."

Nevertheless, Steer's writings about the bombing of Gernika had already been vilified in the United States by a prominent Catholic pen. In a pamphlet published by Father Joseph B. Code with the approval of the archbishop of New York, and with the intention of unmasking the "lying propaganda"[118] that accompanied the Spanish Civil War, a chapter on the "myth" of Gernika accused Steer of having constructed fabricated his story around the bombing.[119] The very fact that these criticisms focused on Steer's work, however, demonstrated how useful it could be for propaganda purposes.

---

117. Letter from Irala to Aguirre, New York, September 3, 1938, in San Sebastian, *The Basque Archives*, 189.

118. Joseph B. Code, *The Spanish War and Lying Propaganda* (New York: Paulist Press, 1938).

119. Cf. Herbert R. Southworth, *La destrucción de Guernica: Periodismo, diplomacia, propaganda e historia*, 2d ed. (Barcelona: Iberia de Ediciones y Publicaciones, 1977), 189.

Out of the rest of the books they showed him, Davin singled out *Le clergé basque* (The Basque Clergy) and *Le probleme basque* (The Basque Problem), but objected that they were "for people who already know the religion well."[120] The American audience was not, at least in this particular, comparable to the European one.

Nevertheless, the delegation did not cease making efforts toward the publication of books that might contribute to swaying American Catholic opinion in the direction of positions more inclined toward those promoted by the Basque government's propaganda. They contacted a variety of publishers about publishing Iñaki de Azpiazu's pamphlet *Siete meses y siete días en la España de Franco* (Seven Months and Seven Days in Franco's Spain), an account of the author's own experiences in the months following the uprising. They met with success, eventually getting the work published by Modern Age.

With Azpilikueta's book, *The Basque Problem: As Seen by Cardinal Goma and President Aguirre*, which the delegation was presumably especially interested in publishing, they had less luck. Scribner's sent it back to them on the grounds that it was not of interest to them. Modern Age repeated the rejection, with the argument that "given the tastes and inclinations of the American audience, this book will not sell." Finally, they succeeded in publishing it with funds granted by the Spanish ambassador, Fernando de los Ríos. Their objective was not to print a large press run, but rather something more modest. It was a matter of printing a limited number of copies for the purpose of selective distribution to intellectuals, the communications media, and particular social groups. Things went quite quickly. By mid-November 1938, the book was already in the distribution phase.[121]

They left *Le clergé basque* at a Catholic bookstore. Much the same took place with the pamphlet titled *El caso de los católicos vascos* (The Case of the Basque Catholics), by Iñaki de Azpiazu. They succeeded in publishing Azpiakzu's pamphlet, with the objective of giving it a particularized and high-quality distribution. In addition, there was a permanent distribution

---

120. San Sebastián, *The Basque Archives*, 98.

121. On November 19, Irala wrote to Aguirre that "we began to distribute the book this week . . . We will try to move continuously, but gradually, so that they don't pile up on the readers to whom we send them." Letter from Irala to Aguirre, New York, November 19, 1938, in San Sebastian, *The Basque Archives*, 222.

of propaganda material, handing out articles published under the most prestigious bylines in *Le Temps* and the *Sunday Times.*

They also found a tool to support their propaganda work in the film *Guernika,* which was useful in their endeavors. In September, they showed *Guernika* at the Basque Center in New York, "amid a great deal of interest." Manu Sota introduced it, describing the bombing in accordance with George Steer's account. "The people," Irala recounted, "applauded a great deal at the parade of the *gudaris,* the flag, and the president's passage." In October 1938, the Spanish version was shown for a week at Cinema Latino in New York. Sometime later, the short was shown at the Roosevelt Cinema for a week, this time in the English version. Although the arrangement called for the box-office proceeds to be divided between the owner of the movie theater and the delegation, the initiative did not bring in a great deal of money. Irala acknowledged this when he wrote in his report that "Financially, we won't do much with it, since they don't pay much, as is natural; what is important in it is the propaganda."[122]

Once the propaganda experiment had concluded, Irala was not overly optimistic in regard to the film's possibilities for the future. It had been useful, but its usefulness was nearly played out: "We haven't been successful. People are tired of seeing things about war, and what happened at Gernika is no longer current; it doesn't attract their attention. We'll try now to rent it to the people at the American Spanish Aid Committee for them to show to their associations. Beyond this, which is not easy, and the Basques in Idaho, we won't be able to do more."[123]

In effect, the interest that the film might excite among the Basques of the American West still remained to be seen. The members of the delegation had occasion to test this in the trip they took to that region at the end of the year. On December 22, 1938, the film was shown in Boise, "in one of the best movie theaters." Subsequently, it was also shown in Elko and Winnemucca.

Finally, the delegation based its activities on lectures. On November 16, 1938, Ramón Sota gave a lecture at Princeton University. Around that time, Irala noted that "we have in view several gatherings of intellectuals at which our problem will be discussed." The following year, Sota also gave lectures at Catholic University in Washington and at Colombia University.

---

122. Letter from Irala to Aguirre, New York, October 17, 1938, in ibid., 208.

123. Letter from Irala to Aguirre, New York, November 19, 1938, in ibid., 222.

Fundraising

One of the chief preoccupations of the delegations that the Basque government began opening in various European and Western Hemisphere countries in 1937 was raising funds to finance the social and humanitarian work the executive was carrying out among the Basque refugees in southern France. By 1938, the social-assistance work done by Aguirre's cabinet in southern France was worthy of consideration. According to a report drawn up around that time,

> Using only their own resources. . . without help from the French budget . . . the Basques maintain thirteen refugee settlements in France and Belgium, housing 3,300 of their compatriots. They provide aid to 3,850 people a day. They are educating more than seven hundred children between six and fifteen years of age in four school colonies. They have a secondary school with 120 students. In La Roserie, near Biarritz, they have set up a model hospital that is the admiration of visitors (more than 350 wounded or ill patients are receiving treatment there). The Basques have likewise opened specialized clinics in Cambo [Kanbo], Berck, Saint-Etienne, and Paris. They maintain 1,600 children with sixty-six teachers and twelve chaplains in England. They have a soccer team that is covering itself with laurels in the Americas, and finally, they have two artistic groups that are very popular in France and abroad: the famous Eresoinka choir (110 singers and dancers) and Elai-Alai (55 children).[124]

In the American society of 1938, however, collecting funds destined for countries or territories at war entailed numerous difficulties. The neutrality laws prohibited sending funds to the *governments* of Spain so that there was no way to turn over the sums collected directly to the Basque government. This legal measure, adopted in mid-1937, forced an immediate freeze on the activities of all the associations that had dedicated themselves during the preceding months to raising money to send to one of the European governments at war. The Basque delegation found itself brusquely confronted with this problem, which posed many difficulties to the implementation of its plan to contribute financially to bearing the social-assistance and healthcare expenses being incurred by the Basque government on behalf of the refugees.

---

124. Report on the activities and functioning of the International League of Friends of the Basques and on the need to sustain it. Taken from Larronde, *Manuel de Ynchausti (1900–1961)*, 94–95.

In mid-1938, the Basque government was no longer a government at war, nor was it included on any registry as an organization directly involved in any military conflict. Once Euskadi's territory had been occupied by Franco's troops, its members had been dispersed around the world in a harsh and painful exile. Nevertheless, it was not inactive. Despite the difficulties posed by exile, Aguirre's executive continued to engage in intense public activity. This activity no longer had any military aspect, however. Most of its budget was focused on the humanitarian work performed by the cabinet on behalf of those evacuated due to the war, who were crowded together in increasingly difficult conditions in camps set up in the south of France. Nevertheless, it was not always easy to find a loophole in the neutrality laws to enable the collection of funds in the United States that had a foreign government as their direct beneficiary. Until 1939, transfers of funds to Paris were justified by the fact that the war was localized on Spanish territory, and France was not a part of the conflict. Following the Nazi invasion, however, the problem became more complicated. Manu Sota explained as much to Irala in late 1939: "Until the month of November (1939), those of us who are collecting the subscription did not need to be registered with the State Department, since the money went to the refugees in France, and that requirement was only applied to those who sent money to Spain, which was a country at war. Since France has been at war, however, those of us who send money to France have to be registered with that Department."[125]

Aware of the difficulties posed by the legislation, the members of the delegation considered various possibilities to make their fundraising aims possible. Irala proposed to the Lehendakari the creation under French law of an association for aid to the Basque refugees, so that the sums collected in the United States could be sent to France in the association's name. Some steps were taken along these lines, but by the end of the year, they still had not come up with an entirely satisfactory solution.

Nevertheless, this did not prevent the members of the delegation from taking advantage of contacts and events of all kinds to take up collections in favor of the Basque refugees. Parties, dances, lectures, donations, and so on: what was urgent was to collect funds. They would figure out later what formula to use so that those funds could be sent to the intended recipients without violating American law. All the same, these collections did not

---

125. Letter from Manu Sota to Irala, New York, November 7, 1939 (Archivo Iñaki Anasagasti, Fondo Delegación EEUU).

enable them, at least at the beginning, to raise great amounts of money. In late 1938, Irala's experience gathered during their first months in the United States led him to be less than entirely optimistic about the possibility of reliance on public collections to raise the funds needed by the Basque government. As he observed in a letter addressed to the Lehendakari,

> The opportune time to ask for money for the Basques among these last has already passed; it was at the time of the struggle in Euzkadi and the destruction of Gernika. The day after the destruction, we could have gotten many thousands of dollars at a single event, but there's no help for that now. The Americans are moved by sentimental impulses of the moment, and this is natural . . . There's been a great deal of soliciting on behalf of Spain. We can only act in the Catholic arena, which has not done anything along those lines up to now. Undoubtedly, this has its difficulties, because we will run into enemies who will work against us unceasingly. Nevertheless, I hope that we will obtain something, but it will also take time.[126]

Despite everything, the delegation would succeed in following years in collecting respectable sums to finance social assistance to the refugees, making use of the customary methods in the United States, but always, nevertheless, with doubts about the viability of that proceeding. A clear expression of this is seen in a letter that Manu Sota sent to Paris in late 1939: "The last subscription, which, as you will know, came to two hundred and change, leads me to wonder whether it might not be necessary to end the drive once and for all. I know that quite a few donors are complaining that it hasn't ended already. Alberto [Onaindia] told me that they have already suspended the Basque Group's monthly contribution, which came to a quarter. You will say what is to be done."[127]

---

126. Letter from Irala to Aguirre, Boise, December 22, 1938, in San Sebastian, *The Basque Archives*, 236.

127. Letter from Manu Sota to Irala, New York, November 13, 1939 (Archivo Iñaki Anasagasti, Fondo Delegación EEUU).

5

José Luis de la Lombana's Trip to the United States of America

Lombana's trip to the United States must inevitably be associated with the work carried out there by the Basque government's delegation during its first months of existence; the coincidence of dates requires this. Both Lombana and the delegates arrived in New York in August 1938, and obviously, their first steps in the city had to be taken in the same social and political context. Their missions were not identical, but to a certain degree, they overlapped. Both the delegation led by Irala and José Luis de la Lombana were called to act on a partly identical set of social groups—the Basque diaspora, the Catholic sectors, the press, institutional circles, and so on—in pursuit of very similar propaganda and fundraising objectives.

The delegation's work was much more extensive and conscientious and conducted in greater depth than that of Lombana. The delegation had more personnel, greater resources, and of course, far more time to carry out its work. While Lombana only spent three months on American soil, the delegation remained there for several years, eventually creating a subordinate delegation in the West. Nevertheless, it is interesting to note that their lines of work were not antagonistic, although, as we will see, there were some differences of opinion; above all, it should be pointed out that their respective reports, judgments, and opinions with regard to American society at the time and the possibilities of having an impact on it with informational work were formulated in quite similar terms. There was harmony.

Lombana's Selection to Attend the Second World Youth Congress for Peace

We do not know exactly why it was José Luis de la Lombana, and not another young member of the party, who was chosen by the EAJ-PNV as its representative at the Second World Youth Congress for Peace. In his report, Lombana limited himself to noting that "the representation fell to me," without providing any complementary information that would enable us to guess at the circumstances of the appointment or the reasons on which it was based. It is probable that his youth—he was twenty-seven in 1938—was a determining factor in his selection, together with his committed *jeltzale* activism, his restless personality, and his proven ability to make his way in the most difficult situations. His solid education—he had degrees in law, philosophy and letters, and business—and his experience in the communications field were also surely not irrelevant: recall that he had worked for the *Heraldo Alavés* and that he directed the daily *Euzkadi* for several months during his time in Barcelona. In the end, we must also add that in mid-1938 he had taken up residence in Barcelona. The invitation, as stated in the report itself, was issued through the Ministry of State (as the Ministry of Foreign Affairs was known at the time), which was then headquartered in the Catalan capital, like the majority of the republican government's bureaucracy. Under these conditions, Lombana would have been one of the few young activists that the party structure had at hand in Barcelona, and his active trajectory made him a suitable candidate to carry out such a mission.

There was one small detail, however, that under normal conditions—not, of course, in the middle of a civil war—would have constituted a nearly insuperable barrier to being named to a mission of this kind: Lombana did not speak English, a fact that enormously limited his ability to communicate in the United States, restricting the potential of his propaganda activities.

The Basque delegation in New York, carefully selected by Lehendakari Aguirre, was made up of men with a perfect command of English, such as Antón de Irala and Ramón and Manu Sota, who had studied at British universities and knew the language of Shakespeare as well as or better than they did Spanish. Their ability to maneuver with aplomb in U.S. society was guaranteed to the highest degree possible. Nevertheless, Lombana was unfamiliar with the language. In fact, his main address at the congress was delivered in Spanish, which did not pose an irresolvable problem, since, as Lombana himself wrote, "through a system of interpreters and headphones, it was translated into French and English at the same time"; it was another matter that this linguistic limitation may have prevented him from making other contacts, informal but not for that reason any less fruitful.

Nevertheless, he was no stranger to French. He probably did not have full command of the language, but he could at least make himself understood. He was able to do just that with no less a figure than President Roosevelt's wife, with whom he had the opportunity to chat briefly following the congress's opening ceremony, explaining to her "in bad French" the tragic situation in which the Basque people found themselves. French was no guarantee of being able to communicate effectively in the United States, but it was a resource for establishing relations within the more privileged and better educated social sectors.

Lombana's communication problem was not a hindrance during the congress so much as when Lombana began his propaganda tour after the conclusion of the event. At the international conference there were facilities for translation and simultaneous interpreting, and taking equivalent measures on the tour meant that the constant company of a translator was indispensable. This too, however, did not turn out to be too much of a problem. The North American Committee designated Francisco Ibáñez to act as an interpreter, and as Lombana himself observed, "he took charge of turning into English each paragraph that I spoke in Spanish."

There is no doubt that Lombana was a good choice. Despite the slight disadvantage posed by his lack of English language skills, Lombana had demonstrated his character and resourcefulness to maneuver with agility and effectiveness in the most adverse situations. He had never flinched in the face of difficulties, and of course, he was not about to do so when it came time to respond to such a stimulating challenge as the one before him. In fact, he set to work as soon as he learned about his appointment to carry out that mission.

Aware of the extraordinary importance of images in effective communication, he contacted Julio Jáuregui, the general secretary of the President's Office, to arrange access to the pictorial material belonging to the Euskadi government's Propaganda Secretariat that was deposited with the Ministry of State. He selected fifty photographs, of which he requested four copies each, with the objective of using them to support his remarks in New York. A misunderstanding caused his order to be delayed, but wasting no time, Lombana, always faithful to his drastic and hard-hitting style, complained directly to the Lehendakari. He took advantage of the occasion to express his doubts about the trustworthiness of the individual in charge of the service, one Díaz de Mendibil, and stated, "in my view, he is someone disaffected to our cause."[128] In a subse-

---

128. Letter from Lombana to Aguirre, Barcelona, July 19, 1938 (Archivo Iñaki Anasagasti, Fondo Lombana).

quent letter, Lombana clarified the mix-up to the Lehendakari, although confirming "the personal evaluation that the mentioned gentleman has earned from me in relation to our cause."[129]

As was to be expected, the pictorial support provided by the propaganda services was extremely useful to his work. Since Lombana was called on, among other things, to discredit those who excused the crimes of Franco's army on the pretext that they were defending Christian civilization and the religious spirit, Lombana sought to demonstrate that the warlord's hosts had thrown themselves with particular fury "against the Basque people, whom they recognize as Catholic." In one section of his report he noted that "with photographic information, I proved how during the war, Euzkadi had experienced absolute respect for and complete freedom of conscience, which then succeeded in partially influencing, by way of the nationalist ministers, the republican government that rules the destinies of what is there called the 'loyalist zone.'"

The Trip from Barcelona to New York

In a Spain mired in war, traversed by the lines of battle and blockaded by hundreds of checkpoints, it was not easy to travel between Barcelona and New York. In addition, Lombana was a wanted man. Recall that he had escaped from the Vitoria-Gasteiz jail in order to cross the border and put himself at the party's disposition in Angelu. Under these circumstances, the idea of successfully crossing the Iberian Peninsula was a pipe dream as far as Lombana was concerned. For this reason, he opted to embark in France. All the members of the delegation did the same. On July 12, 1938, he was issued a visa to leave Spain, valid for a single trip.

On July 29, 1938, he passed through the customs post at La Jonquera and entered France by way of Le Petrús. On August 4, 1938, he embarked at the port of Le Havre, and after a nine-day voyage, he arrived in New York on August 13. He reached New York a few days before the arrival of the three men who had been designated by the Lehendakari to form the Basque government's delegation in the United States.

---

129. Letter from Lombana to Aguirre, Barcelona, July 26, 1938 (Archivo Iñaki Anasagasti, Fondo Lombana).

Lombana's Participation in the Congress: Objectives, Purpose, and Direction

The Main Objective: Propaganda

The objective of Lombana's participation in the congress was eminently a propaganda one. As he noted in his report, the party authorities agreed on his presence at the event "for informational work . . . and in order to establish the party's position with regard to the problem posed in relation to oppressed minorities." It was a matter, then, of publicizing the Basque Country's situation in a forum that, given the expected attendance, could strongly amplify that message on the global level. The message to be transmitted was clear. The greatest possible publicity had to be given to the account promoted by Aguirre's government to explain to the world the tragic situation in which the Basque people found themselves in light of the civil war: a peaceful, Catholic, freedom-loving people who were persecuted and expelled from their homeland by a fascist movement that styled itself as a crusade.

In addition, the event would serve to "establish relations of friendship with young people of other opinions and from different countries," something that could have enormous potential with a view toward opening channels of communication that could eventually serve to help publicize the Basque cause all over the world. Thus, Lombana's mission joined the informational efforts being made by the Basque government and the EAJ-PNV in order to win the sympathy and support of world public opinion.

Purpose and Direction

Attendance at the congress was extensive and represented a very wide range of opinion. "The political parties of almost all the states and peoples, except for the Germans, Japanese, and Italians," were represented. In addition to political organizations, youth associations of a religious nature, especially Catholic organizations such as the Association of Christian Youth (Asociación de Jóvenes Cristianos), also attended.

Lombana's participation, as a representative of the EAJ-PNV, was intended to encompass this double dimension: he was there in his capacity as representative of a political party, but of one that was at the same time a Catholic-inspired voluntary organization. In effect, Lombana categorized himself among the participants who were "political representatives who were Catholic, who expressed themselves along these lines, but accompanying those statements with political ideas."

On the political side, Lombana proudly displayed his status as a Basque nationalist, but he loyally and ungrudgingly accepted his inclusion in the delegation sent by the Spanish Republican Youth (Juventud Republicana Española). What is more, in addressing the issue of national minorities and its reflection in the framework of republican legality, he displayed an attitude of reasonable satisfaction. The solution adopted by the Second Republic with regard to the national problems of Euskadi and Catalonia was, in his judgment, moving in the correct direction. The source of the problem was the irruption of Franco and his supporters, which had cut off the progress of those two nations toward self-government. Lombana was clear and eloquent in addressing this point:

> Does the legal and political problem of national minorities exist in the Republic? No. Euzkadi and Catalonia—hear me well—are not national minorities today, but rather peoples who enjoy their own state structure within the concert of Europe.
>
> Euzkadi had its own history until 1839, the date at which the Spanish monarchy deprived us of the liberty that the Republic restored to us. Under the monarchy, we accepted the terminology of a minority, not as an end, but rather as a means for claiming our rights, as a tactical choice in favor of the lesser evil.
>
> In the Republic, the problems of the minorities are channeled, recognized, and guaranteed by the Constitution, which guarantees co-official languages with the system of bilingualism and freedom of conscience with the practice of tolerance, co-existence, and the recognition of religious freedom. Nevertheless, the fascists have invaded us, and the fact is that totalitarian states use the supposed protection of national minorities as an excuse for their behavior, and then they abolish them. Mola, an insurgent general in the service of Italy and Germany, said, "I will raze Bizkaia; I have more than enough means to do so," and he did as he had said.

Nevertheless, Lombana separated himself from the delegation of young republicans when it came time to select the credential he would have to display at the congress's sessions. The other members of the delegation, which was made up of young people from the Libertarian Youth (Juventudes Libertarias), the Socialist Youth (Juventudes Socialistas), the Republican Youth (Juventudes Republicanas), and the Left of Catalonia (Ezquerra de Catalunya), identified themselves as members of the "Spanish Anti-Fascist Alliance" (Alianza Antifascista de España). Lombana refused that credential "due to my special character as a Basque nationalist" and used the Basque Nationalist Youth (Juventudes Nacionalistas Vascas) credential that he had been given by the EBB.

His ideological and doctrinal positions were in keeping with Basque nationalist orthodoxy of the time. He proposed that the congress declare that "the individual is superior to the state, that fascism means the negation of universality and peace, and that it is, as a consequence, beyond the pale of ecumenism and universality."

In his participation on the congress's commissions, Lombana explained and defended the chief arguments on which the Basque government's propaganda work was based in its effort to win the favor of international public opinion and sectors with ties to the Catholic Church.

> "That Euzkadi did not make war, but rather war was made upon Euzkadi; that it limited itself to using force in defense of peace, when all other resources had failed; and that its Christian spirit always presided over its struggle."

> "That the Catholic clergy of the Basque diocese has been persecuted by the fascists and that over eighty priests have been shot . . . If they say that they are defending Catholicism, why did they try to exterminate it?"

> "During the war, Euzkadi has experienced absolute respect for and complete freedom of conscience, which has then successfully spread in part, by way of the nationalist ministers, into the republican government that rules the destinies of what is there called the 'loyalist zone.'"

In contacts before and after the congress, Lombana threw himself wholeheartedly into his propaganda work, informing anyone who asked about the situation of the Basque people, and correcting the errors of all those whom he considered mistaken or ill informed. The network of contacts built by Lombana was extensive and included both prominent figures in the Catholic world and youth groups and organizations with a certain degree of influence in their respective environments.

With the head of Catholic Action in England, Father Heenan, he maintained an eloquent conversation in which he sought to overturn some of the received ideas with which Falangist propaganda had contaminated a large part of the Catholic world. With regard to the Czechs, who were "unfamiliar with the problem of Euzkadi," he wrote several articles that were published in that country's press.

Seeking Aid for Basque Refugees

Along with the propaganda objective that inspired the trip, Lombana took advantage of the opportunity to solicit support for the Basque cause: moral support, of course, but in the first instance and above all, financial assistance for the thousands of Basques forcibly evacuated from their homeland and made refugees throughout the world.

The fact is that he did not miss even one opportunity to fulfill this goal. He did all he could with President Roosevelt's wife, to whom he communicated "the need for the Americas, and specifically the United States, to help the Basques who are roaming the world and suffering exile in France." Mrs. Roosevelt responded that peace would bring the Basques the justice they deserved, provoking the following comment from Lombana: "A pleasant phrase, but one that means nothing."

When setting up the EAJ-PNV's Extraterritorial Board (Junta Extraterritorial) in New York, a mission for which, as we will see, Lombana was expressly authorized by the EBB secretariat, he charged the activists with the duty of contributing money to the Refugee Aid Committee in France, "half a day's income each month, as a voluntary assessment." In effect, fundraising was one of the board's chief functions as an extraterritorial organization of the party. For this purpose, a committee associated with that of Angelu was established in New York, with the objective of "collecting funds and sending them . . . to the account of Don Doroteo Ciaurritz."

The American Propaganda Tour

Once the congress was over, Lombana was presented with the possibility of joining a trip that two of the members of the delegation—Félix Martí-Ibañez, from the Libertarian Youth of Spain, and Amando del Moral, from the Libertarian Youth of Catalonia—were taking to various places in the United States in order to engage in propaganda in favor of the republican cause in the Spanish Civil War.

The invitation came from the Medical Bureau and North American Committee to Aid Spanish Democracy and had the objective of "publicizing the meaning of the war in Spain." Lombana consulted the party authorities, and they relieved him of the need to return to Barcelona, authorizing him to join the propaganda tour. Even so, Lombana sought the opinion of Basque nationalist activists in New York who, far from dissuading him, strongly encouraged him to join the tour. Having confirmed the lack of objections from the party, he decided to participate in the trip, although he set one condition for the organizers. He was going to participate in the tour, but he "would speak exclusively about Euzkadi." They had no objection, but they warned him that at the end of the trip, they would organize collections, the proceeds of which would be destined for their organization's humanitarian purposes. That was how Lombana began the tour that prolonged his time in the United States by several weeks, enabling him to multiply his contacts and the propaganda effects of his trip.

In the credential letter sent to him by the EBB, its secretary, Luis de Arregui, summarized their expectations with these terse words: "The EBB hopes that you will be able to carry out in those countries a task from which great benefits will follow for the cause of Euzkadi's independence, which we defend."

Friction with the Euzkadi Government's Delegation in New York

In August 1938, Lombana arrived in New York at the same time as the members of the Basque government's delegation were preparing to take the first steps toward fulfilling their U.S. mission. This chronological and geographical coincidence roused suspicions and provoked clashes between Irala and Lombana, despite the fact that they had spoken in Paris before departing about the need for coordinated action.

The first meeting between the two took place on August 25 at the office of the Republic's consulate-general in New York, at the reception offered by the consul for the delegates coming from Barcelona to attend the Second World Youth Congress for Peace. Manu Sota and Irala were present at the event, having accepted the consul's invitation, "in order to be polite." Lombana, who was part of the group sent to the congress by the government of the Republic, was among the delegates. In the notes written by the members of the Basque government's delegation, this first contact is described, and some differences of opinion are already evident.

On a personal level, the relationship was a good one. Lombana was immediately in harmony with his fellow nationalists in the Basque government's delegation, although his vision of the distribution of roles did not seem entirely in agreement with theirs. Lombana told them that "he has credentials and authorization from the PNV to act among the Basques and collect funds," and he communicated to the members of the delegation the invitation he had received from the American Spanish Aid Committee to "make a tour all around the country." At that point, the first clash occurred. Irala and Sota expressed to Lombana "the unanimous judgment of the delegation that duplicative action among the Basques in the United States would be entirely counterproductive." Lombana apparently shared this judgment, but he assigned it to a secondary place, recalling that "he should obey the orders of his party."

From the contents of the note, it is possible to infer that the Lehenda-kari had expressed to his collaborators the intention of forewarning the party authorities about the problems of coordination and image that could result from duplicative activities in the United States. It would not be a good thing for the Americans, especially the Basque-Americans, to find that the EAJ-PNV and the Basque government were acting separately, through different individuals and by means of mutually overlapping activi-ties. Lombana affirmed, however, that he "had no news about the outcome of President Aguirre's meeting with the EBB." They agreed to await news from their superiors and make no decisions until receiving word on this point.[130]

Nevertheless, Lombana noted in his report that he had, in previous conversations with Irala, expressed his opinion that "collecting funds was not a mission that belonged to a government, since its work was of an executive nature, and if it needed funds and could not ask the Republic for them, due to the difficult economic situation, my understanding was that the position of the government, which today has no territory, would not be strengthened in any way by asking for financial resources." The mis-sion there, in Lombana's understanding, was "to make the Basque prob-lem known," and in addition, "to create an organization that could raise funds for the government, but without it taking a visible role under any circumstances."

A few days later, Irala wrote to the Lehendakari to inform him about the matter and urge him to send clear instructions immediately:

> I suppose that by this time, you will have determined this point with the party, even if the news has not reached us. Lombana has a letter from Endara, written after you decided to speak with the EBB and they promised to refrain from making a decision until after the conversation, in which they insist that he act in the party's name, since despite what I said to them, they have a firmly agreed policy of acting in that way. We are getting along very well with Lombana, who realizes the situation, but it would be advisable for us to have set policies. Lombana told me yesterday that he was planning to make a pro-paganda trip of a month and a half around the United States, sponsored by the Spanish Aid Committee, but with independent status.[131]

---

130. San Sebastián, *The Basque Archives*, 78.

131. Ibid., 188.

Three weeks later, Irala again asked for instructions. He alerted the Lehendakari to the fact that "in the United States, action by the party would be very badly received, both among the Basques and among the Americans," and he requested clear orders.[132] Nevertheless, it does not appear that the risks pointed out by Irala ultimately posed real problems. Lombana always showed himself respectful of the Euzkadi government, but he did not let any opportunity pass by without drawing a sharp distinction between the public institution and the party that had commissioned him "to give an account of the work of the Euzkadi government's delegation, the work of which he should facilitate, but without forgetting that the government is one thing, originating in the Euzkadi political parties, even if the nationalists have a majority in it, and the PNV is another, to which patriots are under a very particular and preferential obligation."

In the matter of fundraising, Lombana also defended his own positions that differed from those of Irala. Of course, he was not an advocate of duplicating the Basque government's presence and efforts in the United States, but he defended the thesis that fundraising would be better placed in the hands of organizations controlled by the party than in the hands of the Basque government, because the party might lose control of the latter, but not, obviously—or at least not so easily—of the former. He thought that, "all things being equal, it is necessary to strengthen those party organs that are in our hands, in view of the insecurity of creating others that may or may not be controlled by nationalism tomorrow, and without the need, of course, to set up a superfluous competition." Obviously, Irala was of a very different opinion. In his view, "we cannot ask for money for the Basque refugees, so in general, unless it also goes generally to all, through the only channel that exists today: the Euzkadi government. The reverse strikes me as abnormal and not very serious and with fatal consequences for all."

In the end, Lombana decided to fulfill his mandate and set up in New York a branch of the Basque Refugee Aid Committee (Comité Basque de Secours aux Refugies), originally established in Angelu. It was not a time for debate, but for action, and Lombana had express instructions from the EBB to that end which he was not inclined to leave unfulfilled. Working toward this goal, Lombana appealed to the authority of the party, in a gesture that probably would not be thoroughly understood by the members

---

132. Ibid., 209.

of the delegation. In a letter sent to the delegation, Lombana announced to Irala that the committee was going to be created and that

> I, following the instructions of the EBB and of the secretary of the committee, Don Luis de Arregui, will outline for them the work to be done, and our authorities will then say whether they should act publicly in collecting funds, as I believe, since the exclusive legal representation of Basque nationalism has to be a greater guarantee for the Americans, and that role corresponds to our organization here.
>
> I hope that everyone's understanding will mean that there will be no room for "discreditings" and recourse to legal quibbling. Discipline for all and our patriotism will bear greater fruits for the PNV and for the freedom of Euzkadi that we defend.

In the end, Lombana left the United States, and the members of the delegation continued their work in New York, taking advantage of the infrastructure he had created in fulfillment of the mandate he received from the EBB. A trustworthy account of their relationship with Lombana can be found in a letter sent to Pedro de Basaldua, in Paris, a few days after Lombana embarked for France. In that letter, Irala noted that

> By the time you receive this letter, our friend Lombana will have already arrived there. It would be advisable for you to obtain from the party, as an affair of yours, the report he makes about his activity in America, so that the Lehendakari receives it in its entire extent and *in full*. I suppose that he will speak about us in his report, as is natural. This point interests me, of course, if there is anything in particular. We've gotten along well; we've only had the differences of opinion that you know about from the letters sent at the time, but we haven't quarreled, nor anything close to it. Nevertheless, I will tell you that he has always been a bit "restless," as our compatriots say around here, and it might well happen that a stone cast against us will land on the roof of our illustrious *burukides*.[133]

The matter did not escalate. There were some differences of opinion, and harmony was not absolute, but there were neither overlaps nor duplication, nor were any open conflicts recorded. Lombana fulfilled his mission, and the members of the delegation continued with their difficult task.

---

133. Letter from Irala to Basaldua, New York, November 10, 1938 (Archivo Iñaki Anasagasti, Fondo Delegación EEUU).

The Establishment of the Basque Nationalist Party in New York

One of Lombana's chief actions in New York was the establishment of the Extraterritorial Board of the EAJ-PNV in that city. For that purpose, he had express credentials and authorization issued by the EBB secretariat. This was not an ordinary board, however, but rather a body created in an exceptional situation to carry out very special functions. Along these lines, Lombana entrusted to the newly established board a mission strongly imbued with the propaganda aims that had brought him to visit the Americas.

On the one hand, the board was to act "among the Basques, with the objective that they cultivate the characteristics of the Fatherland." The actions of the New York activists were to be rigorous: the board "shall not allow any Basque to speak ill of his Fatherland, but when faced with incomprehension, it will employ the arguments offered by its patriotic culture and the affection owed to all brothers of the same race." In addition, however, it was also to act "among non-Basque Americans, etc., in order to inform them about what Euzkadi is and what its national characteristics are, in the belief that Euzkadi's freedom is in the will of Basques who wish to be free and in that of the other peoples who acknowledge this." Here also, his instructions were precise and reflected the disquiet that animated the *jeltzales*: the board "shall always carry out maximum propaganda in favor of the party's ideals and shall tenaciously defend the Basque people's attitude toward the military uprising, explaining its origin and consequences and how our organization defended the people's life and peace against the hatred and destruction sown by fascism on all sides." On this point, Lombana expected serious activity and a two-way flow of information. The board should keep the party fully informed about individuals, organizations, and activities that might be of some interest in relation to Euzkadi and for the purpose of publishing propaganda "in English, etc."

Finally, the board was to compile a "census of the race" with the objective of learning "the names of the Basques scattered around the world." Lombana encouraged them to set up a card index in which to record every Basque émigré who might potentially serve as an ally of the national cause. The effort to monitor the diaspora was an aim shared with the delegation, which began to compile a Basque census as soon as it arrived in New York. Lombana's report was an interesting contribution along these lines, as it included an extensive list of Basques who were perfectly recorded with their full names, residences, and when possible, personal evaluations of their political preferences and inclinations.

The report added a detailed set of norms intended to regulate the board's organization and functioning. Worth highlighting, however, are the observations made with regard to the terms in which the administrator of the daily *Euzkadi,* said to be "dependent on and the property of the party and its Supreme Council," was to carry out his task. These passages could be profitably read by the bureaucrats and judges who insist on denying the EAJ-PNV's right to financial compensation for the seizure of *Euzkadi,* alleging that it has not been established that it belonged to that political formation.

Appendix
Lombana's Report

Lombana's report began with a very general analysis of American society at the time, followed by a somewhat more detailed account of the positions held by U.S. citizens with regard to the Spanish Civil War and specifically, with regard to the Basque problem. Whether accurate or not, his evaluations were sweeping. Lombana was a man who preferred clear messages, without qualifications or beating around the bush.

American Society: Distant, Cold, and Simplistic

As far as the description of U.S. society at the time is concerned, Lombana's observations on the attitude taken by Americans to human conflicts are worth mentioning. His observations were governed in large part by the ideas that had taken root in Europe regarding American collective psychology, among which three traits were prominent: lack of concern about the fate of the world beyond the country's borders, extremely simplistic thinking, and the enormous role played by emotion when taking a position. Here is a passage that is particularly representative of Lombana's reflections: "[Americans] are not used to profound thinking, and as a consequence, problems trip them up. Sentimental things attract their attention, human-interest stories, as the journalists say. It's difficult to win them over by appealing to their heads; it's easier to break their hearts. For them, the fact that a people loses its independence is not of any great importance, but the fate of a fatherless child, for example, would cause them concern."

Lombana was especially concerned about the scant interest he noted among Americans regarding political events in Europe. He insisted over and over again on drawing attention to this trait in their collective personality: "Americans, the majority of them, are unfamiliar with not only the Basque problem, but also that of the Peninsula. They don't want to know anything about Europe."

On the topic of the superficiality of the schemata with which Basque matters were approached, Lombana slipped into the report a few ironic comments—sarcasm was one of his strengths: "Things in America," he noted, "become known in a distorted way, and so, for example, if you go to the hippodrome, a theater converted into a fronton where the Basque *pelotaris* play jai-alai, you will see them parade to the rhythm of the toreador song from *Carmen.*" At this point, Lombana deployed all his capacity for irony and took the opportunity to note that, although Americans, in general, were strangers to "not only the Basque problem, but also that of the Peninsula," what was more serious was the fact that the Spanish republicans themselves were also unfamiliar with "their problem." Lombana illustrated his evaluation with a very telling anecdote:

> When we reached [the port of] Le Havre, to embark for America, [the members of the republican delegation] were invited to sing the Riego Hymn, their national anthem, as the other European delegations did, and they couldn't do it, because they didn't know it.
>
> We arrived in America, however, and at Vassar College they received us with the Royal March. They hadn't realized that the so-called national anthem had been changed seven years ago.

All the same, Lombana encountered a society that was not entirely uninformed about the Spanish conflict. Fundamentally, Americans had followed the course of the conflagration in the press and had come to form a reasonably clear idea of what was at stake in the war. Whether that idea was correct, in addition to being clear, was a different question. On the other hand, some of the opinions circulating at the State Department with regard to Spain's international repositioning after the war continue to strike an odd note. Lombana summarized the atmosphere of American society in 1938 with regard to the civil war as follows:

> The war is considered virtually lost for the Republic, lost as a result of a lack of support, which different countries, especially France, England, and the United States, were reluctant to provide due to the revolutionary orientation of its governments, as judged by the Americans. They still talk about a revolution there, instead of a war of invasion . . . There, in the State Department in Washington, they are sketching a solution, on the assumption of Franco's presence, in which France and England receive a piece of the Balearics or North Africa in order to guarantee their routes there, and Euzkadi and Catalonia are also autonomous, one dependent on England and the other on France. They believe that Franco, due to his imperialist orientation, will not accept this formula, but that the other democracies can impose it.

With regard to the Basque case, Lombana was pained by the deep incomprehension of the Basques' motives among Catholic groups: "The American Catholic sector believes that it has been political reasons and perhaps not moral ones that have motivated the Basques to fight on the side of the Republic."

Basques in American Society in 1938 and Their Position with Regard to the Spanish Civil War

The central part of Lombana's report was dedicated to describing and evaluating, in separate sections, the Spanish organizations established in the United States with Basque members, according to whether they acted in favor of the Republic or supported Franco. Specifically Basque organizations operating on American territory were also mentioned briefly. In what follows, we systematize and heavily abridge his observations.

Among the Spanish organizations working in favor of the Republic, the Confederated Hispanic Associations (Sociedades Hispanas Confederadas), headquartered in New York, brought together all the regional associations of Spanish origin established in the United States. Controlled by "labor-union activists," they were not sympathetic to Basque nationalism, which their leaders accused of separating "the elements present in the common struggle against fascism." Their weekly, *Frente Popular* (Popular Front), published "abundant articles against us," following the most intransigent line of the libertarian leftist organizations participating in the conflict. Lombana affirmed in his report that, through the mediation of his travelling companions—well-known as anarchists—he succeeded in putting an end to the paper's invectives against the Basque nationalists.

The Central Spanish Relief Committee was an anarchist organization, also headquartered in New York, which openly defended the position that "there is no war in Spain, but rather a revolution made by them, and that the triumph of the revolution is preferable to war." This organization was also hostile to the Basque government "due to the absence of the anarchists in it."

The Medical Bureau and North American Committee to Aid Spanish Democracy, likewise headquartered in New York, was led by a Protestant bishop, Francis J. McConnell. It was a serious and committed organization—typical of American society at the time—that had collected significant funds destined for humanitarian purposes on the republican side.

The Spanish Central Aid Committee for the Spanish Republic (Comité Central Español de Socorro para la República Española) was an organization directly controlled by the republican embassy in the United States and made up of republicans, under the leadership of the Catalan Pedro Borrás.

All these organizations raised money and sent the proceeds to the Iberian Peninsula to be used for humanitarian purposes.

Meanwhile, Lombana also noted the Spanish organizations acting in favor of Franco. Among these, the National Spanish Relief Association, headquartered in New York, had the objective of raising funds to maintain social-assistance programs and winter soup kitchens. Its chief promoter was a native of Bilbao by the name of Ramón Castroviejo. Its honorary committee was made up of the archbishops of Boston and Philadelphia and Cardinal Dennis Dougherty. It published the magazine *Spain,* in several of whose issues statements "against the Basques" were included.

Finally, Lombana listed specifically Basque organizations. The Basque-American Center (Centro Vasco Americano) of New York was a charitable organization of limited awareness and activity, led by an "apathetic" man who, "although he is working today, lacks constancy." Oddly, Lombana did not have a great deal of praise for one of its chief backers, Valentín Aguirre, an almost mythic figure among Basque-Americans in all latitudes during the first decades of the twentieth century. Aguirre was a very well-known Basque member of New York society who would have occasion to manifest his patriotic enthusiasm when the Lehendakari arrived in New York following his hazardous wanderings through Nazi Europe. Nevertheless, Lombana said of him that "he considers himself a Basque very much in his own way; he is afraid and has relations with the Barcelona government and does not want to draw attention to himself or get caught up in clashes with the Spanish fascists." The reasons for this cautious manner of proceeding were financial in nature, in Lombana's opinion: "he has a banking firm." Lombana did not consider the center an effective platform with a view toward raising money for the Basque government, because, he maintained, it was dominated by "an atmosphere of petty personal disputes," which posed enormous obstacles to coordinated and unitary action.

The Basque Group (Grupo Vasco) was a subsidiary of the Confederated Hispanic Associations (SHC) and was made up of Basques "educated in the arena of labor-union activism, who are still imbued with a syndicalist spirit today and make use of the Basque issue to collect funds that they then turn over to the SHC." Lombana had a very frank meeting with the group's leaders, to whom he spoke "clearly and categorically." What they heard from Lombana, by his own account, "did not please them in the slightest." In Lombana's judgment, this group posed a hindrance to the work of the Basque government's delegation.

Meetings, Encounters, Activities, and Lectures

Due to the difficult situation experienced by the Basques evacuated from Euskadi, who became refugees in southern France or were displaced to Catalan territory following the entry of Franco's troops, the Basque government felt an almost anguished urgency to make contact with the diaspora for the purpose of raising funds from the Basques whom a centuries-long exodus had dispersed around the world, in a gesture of solidarity that might contribute to alleviating the tragic circumstances suffered by their compatriots. Obviously, the EAJ-PNV fully shared this concern, not only because it was the party of which the president of the executive was an active member, but also because a large part of the refugees were affiliated with it.

In addition to the Basques of the diaspora, however, it was also necessary to make contact with all those organizations and prominent individuals capable of understanding and sharing the decisions that the Basque government—and in particular, the party to which its president belonged—had taken in the conflict. The aim, in this case, was twofold: propaganda and fundraising. We have already seen the minor differences of opinion that Lombana had with the members of the Basque delegation as a result of the need to carry out this mission without duplication and overlaps. Despite everything, Lombana made his own contacts, and his report gave a full account of them.

Contacts with Basques of the Diaspora

It is not a question of including here an exhaustive list of the Basques or descendants of Basques mentioned in the report. We can be content for now to note that, as in the case of the government delegation, the diaspora occupied a preferential place in Lombana's contact agenda. He spoke with people of all classes and conditions, but it is worth highlighting his conversation with Laura de Albizu Campo, the wife of the president of the EAJ-PNV in Puerto Rico, who was in prison at the time, serving a sentence in Atlanta on account of her political activism in favor of Puerto Rican independence.

Contacts with Democratic Political Parties

Lombana took advantage of the Congress for Peace to call a meeting of "the various democratic parties of Marxist tenets." The response was noteworthy. He succeeded in bringing together young delegates from seventeen countries in Europe, the Americas, Australia, and even Asia (China and India). He spoke to them, according to his own account, about "what the war had meant in the Peninsula and in Euzkadi. How there had not been a solution there, and how from the first day, there had been a concrete program of government made public to the world through the president's statements in December 1936." In the circumstances of the time, being able to directly and personally provide his own account of what had happened in the civil war to such a wide-ranging audience was a major achievement. The attendees, Lombana indicated, "showed interest, and we agreed to reciprocally inform one another about the activities and organization of the different parties."

Contacts with Catholic Elements

Lombana did not ultimately set up a program of meetings with U.S. Catholics as ambitious and complete as the one that the Basque government's delegation succeeded in arranging. However, he did meet with influential individuals within this important community and attempted to influence them, informing, arguing, giving reasons, and on occasion, nuancing or destroying the received ideas on which their positions were based.

On this point, Lombana's report confirms something that we have already noted above. He found himself among a Catholic community that was divided with regard to the Spanish Civil War, but in which positions favorable to Franco and critical of the attitude adopted by "the Basques" in the conflict were the prevailing ones. Following his explanations and clarifications, some of his interlocutors, such as the lawyer James Cooney, an editorial writer for the Catholic daily *New World*, offered their services to "publicize the upright position that we maintain as Catholics." Others, such as Reverend Yancey, were confirmed in their belief that the American Catholics could not help the Basques, because they were bound up with "the Jews, the Protestants, the republicans, and the communists: that is, the enemies of the Church."

Demonstration at Madison Square Garden

Lombana's report offers remarkable information about this large event, organized by the Medical Bureau and North American Committee. Lombana occupied the podium for five minutes, during which he was able to summarize the message that Aguirre's government was trying to publicize around the world, in order to justify its position against belligerent fascism and in favor of peaceful democracy and co-existence. His remarks were interrupted by applause on several occasions, but Lombana was unable to prevent his being preceded, in one more gesture of folkloric confusion, by "some Seville dances," which obviously had nothing to do with what he was trying to represent.

Lectures in Auditoriums and at Colleges and Universities

The organizing committee for the trip arranged for Lombana to give numerous lectures in various academic forums. Lombana included in his report an extensive account of the places where he spoke, the topics he addressed, and the contacts that his talks enabled him to make with professors and influential personages, with whom it would be advantageous to maintain contact in the future. With regard to his role as a lecturer, it is worth highlighting the number and diversity of the subjects on which he spoke. Only someone with his education and his fearlessness would have dared to give so many lectures on such heterogeneous topics in so short a time.

Like the Basque government's delegation, Lombana carried out his activities in the United States in tandem with the republican embassy. In his case, this synchronization was even more logical than in the case of the delegation, since he was part of the group officially sent by the Ministry of State to the Second World Youth Congress for Peace, in response to the invitation formally issued by the organizing body. Lombana knew Fernando de los Ríos personally, of whom he said in his report that "he had been my professor during my doctoral studies in law, when I was taking political science at the Central University." Lombana observed that Fernando de los Ríos gave an exquisite welcome to the delegation sent by the republican government, expressing particular confidence in the role that the Basque nationalists could play in winning over the American Catholic sectors for the anti-Franco cause. Nor did his perception in this regard vary from that recorded by the members of the Basque delegation: "When he [Fernando de los Ríos] found out that we were in New York, he came by plane to visit us, and I was later at the embassy twice to chat. He likes the Basque issue because it is the only way to gain entry among the Catholic elements."

Recommendations for the Future

Lombana concluded his report with some reflections, grouped under the heading "Work to Be Done," in which he listed the steps that would need to be taken to improve and intensify the propaganda work to be carried out in the United States. Earlier in the report, he had suggested initiatives that might turn out to be useful for intensifying Basque-American relations, such as the sale in the U.S. market of Basque products manufactured by the refugees in France—Lombana took the liberty of pointing out, along these lines, that "in Boston, through Garavilla, there is the possibility of selling sandals with payment in advance"—or the grant of lands by the federal government so that the Basques could work them, on the coast or in the interior, a proposal that Lombana made to "various State Department employees, and the idea seemed like a good one to them."

> In this final section, Lombana explicitly and systematically put on record a series of actions that, in his judgment, could be taken without any difficulty to reinforce the lines of action already being pursued. His proposals included producing pamphlets, giving lectures, selling books, and other propaganda initiatives, including the need to "intensify relations with American Catholics, on the basis of demonstrating that we are solely Basques and that we are not linked either to the Republic or to Franco." This document was signed on November 24, 1938. A few months later, the civil war would come to an end, and the almost immediate outbreak of World War II in 1939 would dramatically overtake the lines of work proposed by Lombana in his report.

The Summary Sent to Javier de Landaburu

Days before returning to Europe, Lombana wrote a letter to Landaburu in which he summarized what had been done on the other side of the Atlantic and concisely expressed the impressions he had received in the course of his mission in the United States. The letter's text has the interest of a sincere report sent to a fully trusted friend and colleague. For good or ill, the missive rigorously and faithfully expressed the true perspective from which Lombana evaluated his trip. Here are its most interesting passages:

> I have been through half the world and spoken with all kinds of people; the majority were unaware of the existence of Euzkadi. When I speak to these Americans about our federalism even within Euzkadi, they like that a great

deal, because with that system they say that they live in a universal democracy, even if the reality is otherwise.

I've spoken at many universities; the students who are at the stage of specializing know something about the subject they are engaged with, but not a word of general culture. People believe that Europe is very far away, that it was always a burden for America, and that they live better without worrying about it. The government does not hold this opinion, but the majority of Americans do. They see the danger of fascism as very distant, and if it were to arrive, they believe that they would defeat it without help from anyone, since they have an autochthonous economy. Social progress frightens them, and don't even mention communism. The Constitution prohibits anarchism, and when you enter this country, you have to declare that you are not an anarchist. The workers have little social education; an organization like "Soli" [ELA-STV, the Basque nationalist labor union] would be something extremely advanced here.

About the war, not much good. People here consider the Republic lost and that a European war could help us to find a solution, and although they consider Franco one more "military man," without any brains, they see that England has begun a policy of rapprochement with Germany, which is in no way favorable for our future and which isolates the United States from England. In the embassy, they breathe this atmosphere.[134]

Clearly, in this portrait of the situation sketched by Lombana following his trip, a pessimistic slant predominated. In his judgment, little could be done in America, very little. Both geographically and intellectually, the United States was far removed from Europe and its social and political problems. Nor could his impressions about the evolution of the civil war have been any more negative. Only a miracle could save the republicans. Everything was lost.

There is one aspect of the letter, nevertheless, that does not fail to attract attention in a text written in late 1938. The Republic, Lombana observed, had no possibility of coming out of the conflict triumphant, but "a European war could help us to find a solution."

Lombana's observation makes evident the extreme care with which the Basque nationalists of that time scrutinized political events on the continental and even global stages. In Europe, significant political movements were underway, movements that, depending on the direction they took in coming months, might lead to an armed conflict. It was necessary to pay

---

134. Letter from Lombana to Landaburu, New York, October 26, 1938 (Archivo del Nacionalismo, LiAU 9-1 R-451/6-1).

attention to those movements, so it seemed to Lombana, because if Franco won the civil war, only the evolution of the European geostrategic scene could offer a life raft to Basque nationalism and its political aspirations for Euskadi.

In any event, things were not going well. Even in Europe, the geopolitical scene was becoming ever more difficult. Great Britain's rapprochement with Nazi Germany, Lombana noted, was "in no way favorable for our future."

Bibliography

Archives

Archivo Iñaki Anasagasti, Fondo Delegación EEUU

Archivo Iñaki Anasagasti, Fondo Lombana

Archivo del Nacionalismo, LiAu 9-1; A161/1-6

Archivo del Nacionalismo, LiAU 9-1 R-451/6-1

Archivo del Nacionalismo, Li AU 9-1, R-527/5-1.

Archivo del Nacionalismo, PNV 362-6

Archivo del Nacionalismo, PNV 326-6

Secondary Sources

Arrien, Gregorio, and Goiogana, Iñaki. *El primer exilio de los vascos. Cataluña, 1936–1939*. Barcelona: Fundación Ramón Trias Fargas, 2002.

Azpiazu, Iñaki de. "Prologue." In *El caso de los católicos vascos*. Buenos Aires: Ediciones Egi-Alde, 1939.

Barandiaran, José Miguel de. *La guerra civil en Euzkadi: 136 testimonios inéditos*. Milafranga-Villefranque: Bidasoa, 2005.

Code, Joseph B. *The Spanish War and Lying Propaganda*. New York: Paulist Press, 1938.

Fox, Soledad. "Misión imposible: La embajada en Washington de Fernando de los Ríos," in *Al servicio de la República: Diplomáticos y guerra civil*, edited by Ángel Viñas. Madrid: Ministerio de Asuntos Exteriores y de Cooperación; Marcial Pons Historia, 2010.

Irujo, Manuel. *Un vasco en el Ministerio de Justicia*. Buenos Aires: Editorial Vasca Ekin, 1976.

Larronde, Jean-Claude. *Exilio y Solidaridad: La Liga Internacional de Amigos de los Vascos*. Bilbao, 1998.

Larronde, Jean-Claude *Manuel de Ynchausti (1900–1961). Etorri handiko mezenas bat: Un mecenas inspirado.* Translated by Susana Preboste Iraizoz. Milafranca-Villefranque: Bidasoa Historia Garaikideko Erakundea, 1998.

Olondriz,Javier. "Introduction," in José Echeandia. *La persecución roja en el País Vasco: Estampas de martirio en los barcos y cárceles de Bilbao; Memorias de un ex cautivo.* Barcelona, 1945.

Pablo, Santiago de. *En tierra de nadie: Los nacionalistas vascos en Álava.* Vitoria-Gasteiz: Ikusager, 2008.

Pablo, Santiago de. *Tierra sin paz: Guerra civil, cine y propaganda en el País Vasco.* Madrid: Biblioteca Nueva, 2006.

Raguer,Hilari. *La pólvora y el incienso: La Iglesia y la Guerra Civil española (1936–1939).* Barcelona: Península, 2001.

Ruiz Manjón, Octavio. *Fernando de los Ríos: Un intelectual en el PSOE.* Madrid: Síntesis, 2007.

San Sebastian, Koldo. *The Basque Archives: Vascos en Estados Unidos (1938–1943).* Donostia-San Sebastian: Txertoa, 1991.

Sierra Bustamante,Ramón. *Euzkadi: De Sabino Arana a José Antonio Aguirre: Notas para la historia del nacionalismo vasco.* Madrid: Editora Nacional, 1941.

Southworth, Herbert R. *El mito de la cruzada de Franco.* Paris: Ruedo Ibérico, 1963.

Southworth, Herbert R. *La destrucción de Guernica: Periodismo, diplomacia, propaganda e historia.* 2d ed. Barcelona: Iberia de Ediciones y Publicaciones, 1977.

Tapiz, José María. *El PNV durante la II República (Organización interna, implantación territorial y bases sociales).* Bilbao: Fundación Sabino Arana/Sabino Arana Kultur Elkargoa, 2001.

Tierney, Dominic. *FDR and the Spanish Civil War.* Durham, NC: Duke University Press, 2007.

Tusell, Javier and Garcia Queipo De Llano, Genoveva. *El catolicismo mundial y la guerra de España.* Madrid: Biblioteca de Autores Cristianos, 1993.

Zapatero, Virgilio. *Fernando de los Ríos: Biografía intellectual.* Valencia: Pre-Textos, 1999.

Index